American Road Runner

By:

Bob Marshall

Copyright © 2018

By: Bob Marshall

Published By: American Road Runner Publishing

All Rights Reserved. No part of this publication may be reproduced or transmitted in any form or by any means electronic or mechanical. This includes photocopy, recording, or any informational storage or retrieval system without written permission from the Author.

You may contact the Author at:

Americanroadrunnerthebook@gmail.com

Instagram: Americanroadrunner

Facebook: American Road Runner

Website: www.americanroadrunnerthebook.com

We recognize that some words, model names and designations mentioned herein are the property of the trademark holders. We use them for identification purposes only.

Library of Congress Control Number: 2018914720

Reference: 1-7328619-1-9

ISBN; 978-1-7328619-2-3 Hardback
ISBN: 978-1-7328619-1-6 Paperback
ISBN: 978-1-7328619-0-9 Ebook

Bob Marshall

American Road Runner

Photography

By:

Twila Knight Photography

And

Bob Marshall

Cover Art

By:

BOMONSTER

All Rights Reserved

Bob Marshall

DEDICATIONS:

For My Children:
Who taught me unconditional love

For my Pops:
Who never gave up on me

For Lorri Barisic:
Our fallen Queen of the Stampede

For My Fellow Stampeders:
For all the miles of competition

Prologue

Years ago, I started competing in the cross-country chopper race known as The Stampede. It's all about running on a stripped-down rigid motorcycle as fast as you can from left to right here in these United States of America. The first time I ran this race I learned a lot, with most of my engine blowing up somewhere in the middle of Texas and my 30 something year old body breaking down. It all showed me just how many questions I had to answer to get to where I wanted to be in this underground world of racing. That year I still managed to come in 16th out of almost 40 competitors; racing 3000 miles in just over 3 and a half days, mostly on half an engine.

This is illegal, outlaw, unsanctioned road racing with 4 rules: no windshields or hard bags, no chase vehicles, no soft engine mounts and rigid frames only, meaning: no shocks in the rear. My machine had to be able to take the punishment of all the road had to offer. I chose to build around a retired cop moto from the streets of San Francisco, manufactured by Kawasaki as a KZ1000 Police model. I got the inspiration to build on this platform from my Pops who owned an old 1959 Harley Davidson cop bike he had chopped up when I was just a little dude. Retired cop bikes have seen a lot; if they made it through that service, they should be ok with all the adventure and punishment the Stampede had to offer.

I put around 300 loving hours into rebuilding my cop bike to qualify and compete in this race. Asking my old machine, my aging body and my spoiled American attitude to run far and fast was a tall order. Compound that with all the danger the open road has to offer, and the greatest danger of them all, myself. The question was simple: How fast can a common man like me race his home rebuilt machine across this country while dealing with all that everyday life has to offer?

At 38 years of age, I am competing again in the greatest illegal cross-country chopper road race to ever exist in the history of man. I can write this because most people could not or would not lower their standards enough to compete in such machine abusing, body destroying and soul stealing debauchery. This kind of badassery is frowned upon by the masses and reserved for the unethical and immoral types like me. With 60 or so competitors the year the story in this book took place; the Stampede would leave the desert town of Barstow California, ending in Southern Pines North Carolina - without stopping. We all would take the same secret route given to us just 12 hours before the flag dropped at 6 am on the Sunday known to the rest of the world as, Father's Day.

When I competed in this race before, I was married. Now divorced, running in this race and finding a new road in my middle-aged life would prove to be a great adventure of self, against self, with self and for self, just as completely selfish as one could be. Wrenching, rebuild, road running, and racing is one of the most selfish things I do, right up there with taking the time to write this book. Just time to myself to think, breath, create and find the answers to my questions, my way; all while pushing myself and my machine across this beautiful country. This book is very real, and it all took place. Some of the names of the people in my life have been changed to protect their anonymity but other than that please note that I am just not creative enough to make this shit up.

We are all members of the human race; so race we must!

Enjoying a cigarette in my mouth, coffee tumbler in one hand and throttle in the other, the morning air kisses my face reminding me that no matter what the weather brings, it's going to be a beautiful day out here on the road. Always doing my best to make said road beneath me mine; running on it, enjoying it, moving with purpose all while staying alive and accepting all the adventure that ensues astride one of my many motorcycles. When I am moving as fast as I usually do, many hundreds of miles can be covered in a day.

The land and weather, along with the road, can change drastically. It could open up and hail on me or I could climb enough in elevation and find snow. The heat could find me and penetrate everything; feeling like every ex-girlfriend is holding a hair dryer at every part of my body. Bumps, cone zones, bad cage drivers and detours are all just part of the experience. Sometimes I stop on my road to find answers to questions only to find more questions that need answers. It seems the more answers I find, the more questions find me. It all reminds me that questions worth answering, are figured out running on the road astride a 2 wheeled machine.

I still live and work as a mechanic in Riverside, California where I was born and raised. My house is here, right across the street from the house my Pops owned when I was born. My children are here, so there is no reason to get too far from those adorable creatures. I still run a family race team of Land Speed and Flat Track racing with my son. I have not moved very far, but when that mistress, the road, calls to me I run to her with two wheels spinning beneath me.

This story takes place in only a few days of my life, but priceless time it turned out to be for me. I spent about 2 years putting into words the badass, self-defeating challenge known as

The Stampede. It's no different to me than rebuilding a skoot or anything else I enjoy; this book just took a lot longer to complete. I am always tuning myself and my relationships with the people and things around me. My life has to suit me, as I see fit, fulfilling my happiness as an American. Running road and writing about it is just what I do for myself.

A side story to this book is that my Pops would start to edit it for me. This made it, like my motorcycle racing team, a family affair that comes with all the ups and downs of business with family. One day in the summer of 2017, I would be sitting in a hospital room with my Pops in Downey, California. We had spent that whole week together in and out of different hospitals while he went through emergency triple bypass surgery. The man had a heart attack a day before even going to the hospital, but he was being good, doing everything the doctors and nurses told him to do. In that week, we would rewrite and edit a lot of the first few chapters of this book, enjoying the time together as father and son can while doing our best to keep up with his new change of physical health. As he was enjoying reading a book to me called 'The Man Who Would Stop at Nothing' by Melissa Holbrook Pearson, he would suffer a massive stroke in a recovery room, with no one else around us and die in my arms at 66 years of age.

As you will learn, my Pops was simply always there. Just a big influence on my life, in all I do. He was always following me on his newer, 'old man bagger' of a skoot, with his unwavering love and support for all I did and all we got to enjoy together. But that, as they say, is another story. I have moved a lot around in my life since this story took place but at the end of the day, I am just a man with a passion to race. Running on road while enjoying the adventure of it all. Life moves by pretty fast, so I might as well race it. Everyone has a story, thanks for enjoying some of mine.

American Road Runner

Bob Marshall

Bob Marshall

#1

Astride my old chopped motorcycle riding north on interstate 15 after leaving the quiet town of Barstow, California. My good friend F Bomb is riding next to me. We are moving along at a steady 60 miles an hour, inhaling the cool dry air the desert only gives you around here at 6 in the morning, this time of year. It's Father's Day and I bet my kids wish I was home, but instead I am out here in the wind. Everything else feels right around Bomb and I, including the thunderous noise in our ears and pulsing vibrations to our bodies. It all consumes us with an energy immeasurable and completely unthinkable by the human mind. We move slow and steady, taking it easy for a few miles, letting all the lubricants and the internal parts of our righteous skoots warm up proper. They will, after all, be running straight and hard for the next few days - without stopping. Personally; I just put this old engine back together, so with only a few hundred miles on it, I would hate for it to blow up on me now. My machine is not glorious or pretty, but I built it for me and just for this. It's an old Kawasaki moto patrol cop bike from the streets of San Francisco and I dig every ugly square inch of it. Bomb is astride his own custom build jobber known as 'The Miss Lorri.' It's a smaller Harley Sportster rigid frame with a Honda Rebel 250cc engine set as its power plant, moving it along nicely. With its oversized gas tank, it gets so many miles to the gallon that it goes longer between fuel stops than any other skoot and has a low café racer style stance. Damn, it's a true work of art with all its paint and metal work. All touched and graced with Bomb's mechanical genius, that is; except for the inside of the old 1985 engine that has never been cracked open or tampered with. It's totally original. It whines and sings next to me like only a little Rebel engine could.

As we ride, we are surrounded by 60 or so other riders on their chopped machines all quickly passing us by with a grave urgency to get in front of one another. Smashing gears, twisting throttles and taking chances, they are running hard. Bobbin' in and out of traffic, revving engines higher and higher, all elbow to elbow on this road. It is one of the greatest sights, smells, and sounds to ever be experienced as Bomb and I kick back to take it all in.

We are all in an un-sanctioned, illegal, cross country, west to east, winner takes all, chopper road race known as: The Stampede. We can be seen for miles and miles as the road gradually rolls on. Some of the toughest working, playing, wrenching, and riding group of men and women ever known, running fast and hard. Our chopped skoots are old and new, handmade, re-made, over made, under financed, you name it; all roaring with one common goal: to finish this race, and for many, finish first.

This IS a race, and, it's all about THE RACE. This is the greatest race I could've ever imagined, and it is very real, unfolding right in front of me. There are a few rules and regulations but it's very simple: you start on the left side of the country and finish on the right with 3,000 miles of road between. The first one there wins it all. With a designated handwritten route on a sheet of standard paper handed out to all who passed inspection and ponied up a 50 spot just 12 hours before the flag dropped this morning, all this awesomeness began.

Soon it will be just me out here. Me and my homebuilt, rebuilt machine working and fighting with the weather, people, land and road. For me, this time in the saddle is much needed. With a lot on my mind from my children, my family, my new girlfriend, the girlfriends we share, some ex-girlfriends, my ex-wife and a mistress, yeah, I am a man with a few things weighing me down and I have 3,000 miles to straighten it all out or leave it in the wind.

We are all members of the human race; so race we must!

In the end it has to be all about me, surviving and thriving as a member of said race, conquering all the great dangers and challenges of life while astride two wheels. Totally exposed on my machine out here on the road leaves me dodging danger and making decisions to keep me alive. It's all a game with no extra quarters. Game over means -- game over. The biggest challenge will be to survive the most known danger of them all, myself.

Like everyone else competing, I have spent a great deal of time, money, blood, sweat and energy to get running in this race. Taking two weeks off from work at my government job as a mechanic was easy enough, my boss is just that cool and supportive of what I do. The time away from my children, home and responsibilities is never easy. I had to ready my machine, my gear and have all the details taken care of by the time the flag dropped. It was a journey, before the journey began, just to make it to the starting line. I could not have done it without the support of family and friends. So here I am; running and competing with F Bomb right next to me.

American Road Runner

For this quick moment, I take in all the glory of the weather on this beautiful morning and the fabulous road, rolling on just inches beneath my feet. That righteous feeling that I am privileged to be a part of this, immersed in the here and now. Flying on this semi-smooth interstate, leaving it all behind for a while or maybe, I am carrying it, and so much else, all with me. Only time will tell, and the questions will have to be answered.

I take my left hand off the grip and reach forward to push in my home-built cigarette lighter, whipped to my handlebars with a piece of leather. Reaching down into the tank bag in front of me, I maneuver my fingers around a bit with my riding glove on and find my cigarette pack, slowly pulling a smoke out. Lifting my snap on face shield, the wind hits my face and I place the smoke between my lips. I look down to see my lighter has popped up. I pull it and hold it to my smoke, drawing my breath in. Moving my head to the left, I take a quick glance of myself in my rear-view mirror, seeing it has lit. I see that look on my face, that one questioning look we can only give to ourselves. I am going to have to answer some of the questions in that look, and soon. Pushing that aside for now, it's time to go. Time to get my giddy on. Although the Miss Lorri bike moves at a good klick, its 250cc power plant cannot move with the speed my punched out 1000cc can. Soon I will have to unleash the horses of this engine between my legs and let it fly just as I rebuilt it to do. Placing the lighter back in its holder, I hear a thought in my head crystal clear, "Ya need to quit this smoking someday Bob." I leave the smoke in my mouth and rummage around in my left vest pocket till I find my mp3 player. My earbuds are already in my ears, something I have to do before I put my helmet on, and right now it is time to press play.

Ozzy Osbourne. "I Don't Want to Stop." *Black Rain,* Epic Records, 2007.

"All my life I've been over the top, I don't know where I am going but I don't want to stop," I yell to myself in my face shield. Looking over at Brother Bomb with a smile ear to ear across his big face, barely able to be made out under his full-face helmet. He nods with his long dark hair flapping in the wind, he looks excited as a schoolboy to be riding on this road. I give him a left hand thumbs up and a wave while twisting my throttle a little more. He waves back in that grand 80's gesture, pumping his fist in the air like a spectator at a heavy metal concert, a true gesture of the hardcore that is this; cross country chopper racing.

Riding on squirrely choppers cross country can be a dangerous way to travel, people have died doing this. My mind will have to clear and get straight if I want to finish this alive. I scream back to Bomb, pumping my fist in the air. With a swipe of my left hand my face shield slaps down as I scream into it, "Fuck yeah, it's go time, Go Bob, Go!"

Twisting my throttle and winding up my engine I check for clear traffic and lean to the left, shifting this beast into top gear, feeling it kick and pull forward. I know it will be several days before F Bomb and I see each other again. We both accept that we have a demanding adventure in front of us, even though we have both done this before; him many more times than me. This time we get to do it better, our way. The way we want to ride and compete in this race with more wisdom under our belts and more tricks up our sleeves. My bike still pulls as I give it just a little more throttle up this road with power to spare.

I never know exactly how fast I am going as I took the speedometer off years ago. I'm really just interested in how the engine is running and how the bike feels with the weather and road. Some might say it has to do with not being bothered by Johnny Law, but let's face it, if you pay a little attention all around it is pretty easy to guestimate miles per hour. I do have my tachometer telling me how fast the engine is spinning in revolutions per minute, or RPMs. I mounted it down next to my gas tank and it sits just inside my right knee. If I want to see it, I have to take my eyes off the road and look down, so I rarely see it. While I am thinking of it though.... I am holding steady at 5.5 thousand RPMs, right where I want to be. Right where the designers who engineered and manufactured this machine intended for it to be. My engine is pumping along, buzzing in only a way this inline 4-cylinder J style engine can. All else feels and looks good with my machine; with me mounted upon it, controlling it, navigating it, it is MY Bitch. And right now, MY Bitch is good.

Catching up with the long drawn out pack in front of me now, Bomb is in my rear-view mirror. He is tucked into his bike with his left hand on top of the tank while his right hand holds the throttle. He looks absolutely one with his machine, it is an awesome sight to witness as the road bends a little to the right. My one rear mirror view, shaking and rattling at this speed, does not do this sight justice. I set my throttle lock lever, detaching my body from the bike for a quick moment, turn half around to the right and my head the rest of the way, just to witness this in real time. Bomb has many visible miles of road stretching out behind him, a late starter passing him, and just a quick hand wave between them. He is a man in his element, his place of Zen, absolutely relaxed on his steady moving machine rebuilt by his own two hands. There is a lot to be learned seeing the awesome sight of man and his machine. He is on the road, at one with his surroundings and accepting his situation in the slow lane; completely comfortable and in tune while totally concentrating on moving forward. I take note appropriately. Bomb may be my friend, but I was a fan of his before we were friends. Ten years my senior, I pay attention to his actions every chance I get, learning many things with my curious observations. It has always amazed me how much can be learned by observing when taking the time to stop and actually observe. So many of us in this crazy world these days are too busy doing things by the book, we don't always take the chance to SEE what's right in front of us and learn from what we observe. Bomb is one hell of a wrencher, road runner and racer. Lucky me to call him my friend.

I turn my head back to the road in front of me and wherever my head goes, my body tends to follow. Astride my skoot it feels no differently than a pair of shoes on my feet. It is all simply just an extension of me; and the me right now is moving in a small hurry to compete.

For the next several days, this will be my universe. Alien invasions or World War III could be going down and I would not know of it. The road is my task, this road is my journey. It's my adventure for the taking, my path of travel, and I will be making it mine appropriately. This adventure that lays in front of me is simply unknown and endless. I am racing on this, the great American roadway that my taxes have been paying for, built on the backs of my forefathers under a President's New Deal to get us rolling on asphalt and the contracts of hard labor that followed. I am sure those people would all believe what we are doing is pretty darn cool, but the element of danger is very real and staring me right in the face like the black bandana of death I have tied around my handlebars. Passing a few slower moving big rigs reminds me, The End - is everywhere. I am confident I can work with my environment and avoid death and, will have to keep up that confidence or suffer the consequences.

I pass a slower moving old Harley with a 4-speed transmission and its rider pushing it hard. I've got to give him a lot of credit. For him, it's more a question of IF he will finish, not necessarily if he finishes first. Very cool of him and his righteous old machine. I was raised around a similar machine my Pops had when I was just a little dude. I take in all the glory of that chopper and the desert behind it on this glorious American road.

#2

A few miles into the race, some of the really fast competitors are already miles ahead of me. Hell bent, wound up tight, and long gone…gunning for an early lead at any cost. They can't be seen, and will not be seen, until the other side.

The start line this morning was a gathering in the parking lot at the old California Inn on Main Street in Barstow, just a few blocks from the interstate. We all lined up and took off at 6 a.m. sharp in a mayhem of fury to be in front of one another, which caused a few of us to collide at the bottleneck of the driveway. My skoot got hung up on another, causing them to stop while I accelerated. He fell into me a little and I got to put my feet down. It was all simply a little rubbing with my morning coffee and that's what we call, 'Racing.' The racing reality is wrapped around me and I, for one, won't be letting a little rubbing slow me down. Street signs and signal lights be damned, everybody ripped and roared down the Main Street hitting the freeway as a thunderous pack of earth-shaking machines gunning for first place. F Bomb and I were happy to rip out of the parking lot, but we just cruised along when we hit the interstate, watching it all unfold in front of us. What spectacle and mayhem this motley crew of racers knows how to put on!

American Road Runner

My friends and family may not be too happy to realize things like rubbing can, and will, happen during a race, but my Pops understands completely what I am doing. He is happy to lie for me and assure the rest of them I will come out the other side alive. I had to spend the last several weeks reassuring my girlfriend Ella that everything would be fine. I have, after all, done this before and even though we refer to this as a race, it's just a cool ride cross country on our old beat up choppers. Yeah, it's not that; it's a race. At the starting line I could see a little fear in her beautiful dark eyes and questions on her youthful face. At 12 years my junior, she is 26, tall with long dark hair, long legs and a smile that would keep sailors at bay. But here I am leaving her in California with my Pops while I race away. Damn I will miss her, her soft warmth, and large breasts while out here on this cold hard road but that is the price of this adventure. As a solution, I have already purchased her a plane ticket. She is all set to meet me on the other side at the finish line in 4 days. She should be fine while I am gone.

My son has a different view of the race. That little dude watched me pour a lot of time and effort into getting all this together. He is always right beside me, eager to learn and wrench with me. It is my hope that my lifestyle of greasy hands, dirty skoots and racing don't scar him too much, rather that it bestows upon him a sense of problem solving and maybe gets him into some good summer work and keeps him in school. At 9 years old he is still young enough to think me, his old man, cool. One day he may not think so, but for now it's all good quality time we had wrenching on this skoot and then, I leave for 2 weeks to go off and race. This always leaves me wondering why I can't just be like all the other regular dads. Why can't I just sit around in my slippers and smoking jacket, watching television in my big chair, weeding the garden on Saturday mornings, maybe drive all the neighborhood kids down for some ice cream. The simple answer is, I do most of that except the sitting around part, I rarely sit. Oh, I own a T.V., it's hooked to the V.C.R. in a corner of the living room behind the doors of a cabinet. Once a month we might sit down to enjoy a classic western movie but for the most part I am always running and doing, keeping busy twiddling wrenches and rebuilding machines. I hope all this adds up for a good childhood for him and that our time together is not wasted. I have to hope he has fond memories of his squirrely dad doing crazy shit, all in the name of never growing up.

Within a few miles, I start to see some fellow competitors stopped on the roadside. I rubber neck a little but don't recognize any of them or their machines as I fly by. They seem to mostly be on their cell phones, calling for assistance while one or two of them are kicking their shiny machines. Darn I hate seeing machines being kicked like that. There are really only two types of machines or mechanical devices in this world: those that will break, and those that are broken. There always seems to be a few people in every crowd happy to kick and blame the machine for their mechanical misfortunes, we all know them, or maybe once we were them or, we are them. Regardless, they pushed their machines too hard in the first several miles and the road gremlins came out and, in turn; their machines gave out for one mechanical reason or another.

One of the rules of this race is we, the competitor, cannot have anyone chasing us. There is no assistance allowed from others behind us with a truck and trailer full of tools to pick us up. If you get a tow or end up in a shop on route; that's cool but those are strangers, friends or fans offering you a service, not your own personal mechanic chasing you in an air conditioned rig, pulling a box trailer with your name on it. With the spirit of this rule it is included that we, the fellow competitors; do not stop and assist. We all have great respect for each other in what we do and how we do it but, racing IS racing, right now these people are my competitors. I give a small wave and keep flying.

Enjoying the smell of the calm desert interrupted by burnt oil and rich fuel mixtures, my morning coffee and some tobacco smoke. I can't help laughing into my face shield, remembering a time several years ago when I actually DID pull over in the middle of Texas to assist a fellow competitor, a man known as, The Grandpaw. He broke down on the side of Interstate 10 which, can get so long and straight in the middle of Texas that I was able to see him for miles ahead of me. He was rummaging through his tools he carried in old fanny packs strapped to the spare fuel cell rack on the back of his old Harley shovel rigid. I pulled over in front of him and dismounted.

"You aren't supposed to stop!" Grandpaw yelled at me in his northern accent over the big rigs whizzing by us. Now, you have to know that I had just met Grandpaw a day earlier at the start of this race. My Pops was there and introduced us. They both started chatting it up as Grandpaw's old Harley shovel was torn apart in the parking lot of the motel for one reason or another. It may seem strange to do this without a garage around, but for us racers, it's just part of what we do and a common reality. We just always carry enough tools to rip our machines down as needed for maintenance or repair - it's clothing and personal hygiene products we have trouble with. So, my Pops is just that type of man who can walk up and talk to anybody, especially about old chopped Harleys, as I mentioned, he owned one when I was a little dude.

Grandpaw himself is a retired miner from the furthest most northern parts of Minnesota. He is well built and lean and if you did not notice his grey hair, you would think he was in his early

30's. You would also think he was getting ready to kick your arse if he did not smile at you through his thick glasses. He is just that cool and always sporting red Chuck Taylor's on his feet. I was a big fan of his riding and home rebuilt machines, mostly older shovel and knucklehead Harleys with Suicide clutches and simply beautiful paint jobs that can easily be found in a crowd. He really is kind of a living legend in this race and the chopper world in general.

"Well I know," I finally replied to Grandpaw, "I just wanted to make sure you got enough water and coffee and the like?"

"Oh, I am fine!" Grandpa yells back, "I have a flask of espresso shots, that's plenty to drink till the tow truck gets here. My smokes are good as the last gas station had the non-filtered kind I like. I think I blew my back cylinder; the race is over for me kid. I'm getting towed back to that town about 30 miles back, Seguin I think it was called. I'm goanna buy a truck or something and we will see you at the finish line. Your time in this race is good young man, now get out of here before someone sees you, I'll be fine!"

"Yes Sir!" I ran back to my machine, remounted and hauled ass out of there. What a wakeup call that was; this man, Grandpaw, has got to be in his late 60's, he has been at this for years and made it this far. Why the heck would I ever think he would need any assistance from me? After that race we met up at the finish line and he thanked me for pulling over. Since then, I have learned it's best to pull beside, or in front of fellow riders on the side of the road and, throw a thumbs up and see what their response is. This gives them the chance to stay focused if needed on their roadside repair or, ask me for assistance without having to yell "Hey, I'm fucked, can you help me please?"

Lesson learned from one of the great old timers; the man from the north known as The Grandpaw.

Reckless Kelly, "Wicked Twisted Road." *Red Dirt,* Sugar Hill, 2005.

Back to today's race, my new android phone is mounted on the handlebars in a ridiculous looking rain proof case. I can see posts popping up on social media from friends stating that, "Competitors are falling out and breaking down south of Las Vegas and can anyone NOT in the race assist them with a tow or parts, etc." Weird...I just past those broken-down guys; one with tools in hand on his knees but the others, simply on their phones. I can only imagine the stress of breaking down on your motorcycle in the desert with so many other competitors flying by. Maybe they got no sleep last night and were too tired to make rational decisions like: "Shit my skoot is dead, better get my tools and start a fixin' on it so I can get back in the race!" Or, "Time for me to go through the process of elimination and see what I can figure out the problem!" Then it occurs to me; maybe they just don't think that way? I have learned the hard way in my short life that I think, process, and dispatch almost everything, very differently from others. Be it my upbringing, or my right-brained, left-handed thinking; maybe an over attention to detail in my hyperactive disorders. I just process it all very differently than most and have to be careful not to offend those around me with my problem solving. Gotta let a man do his work his way and give these 'dead on the side of the road' racers a lot of credit for showing up and jumping into the arena. Credit will always be given to the man in the arena, win, lose or draw. Who knows, they all still might find their way back into the race yet, that's all part of the sport we play while running on this road.

Bob Marshall

I've always been one to thinks it's okay to take a few minutes and get to know your machine. If it fails, and you just pull over and call someone for help, you have not solved a damn thing. All you did was spend money on a tow. I will be thinking and pondering these ideas for the next several days... why not? There is time, real time to think, ponder; live and breathe as a human man while hauling some serious arse on my skoot. Also, from here on out, let's just simply refer to the motorcycle machine between my legs as a skoot. It is easier that way as so many people try to define this-type of motorcycle from that-type but, in the end; it's got two wheels and an engine with a few things in between: it's a skoot!

Reaching forward for my phone, I scroll through it carefully with one eye. I take a picture with the desert behind me and post it to social media. I think it includes my location as well. Now everybody should be able to figure out where I am and that I am making good time. This may sound easy enough but with the rigid frame of a chopped skoot comes small sacrifices like; a stable or cushy platform to take pictures. Everything is vibrating and undulating violently. I can take my left hand off the bars simple enough but finding the buttons on the phone is work, that is; very hard to steady my hand enough to do so. I accomplish this mostly by burying my elbow in my chest against my riding vest, so the distance of my arm is less to navigate to the buttons on my phone. Oh, and I cannot forget to pay a little attention to the road. I bet I could actually be cited and fined for this kind of nonsense.

These handlebars are new to my skoot. I picked them up a few months ago at the Long Beach motorcycle swap meet, a $15-dollar score. They replaced my old set of ape hangers that got mangled when I flew over them in the last race; that's another story. These 'new-to-me' bars used to be chrome and needed some welding on but turned out to be just perfect for me as I caress them and hold them tight. Leaning back just right, they spread perfectly for my shoulders and arms. As I grip them, they remind me of that perfect set of hips on that perfectly built woman for my wide shoulders. My helmet and a corner of my face are in that picture and Immediately get a lot of responses and comments of good wishes. Oh, all the fun that can be had with friends on the open road; gotta love this social media magic.

This road stretches out before me, seeming to have no beginning and no end. I know it is mine and I will make it so, astride my skoot with the wind covering me in kisses while the land surrounds me as a reminder that I am home. This is my home as -- this is my choice to compete and conquer this road in all its glory. It is all mine, I will run it my way, for my reasons, my road!

#3

"GO BOB, GO!!!" is the term I will mutter, yell and scream to myself the next several days. My skoot is performing in the most superior manner imaginable; this is no mistake. All my hours of engine work, frame welding, chopping, fabricating and moving this machine around to fit me is all part of the plan. With so many hours invested in this machine, I know it inside and out, very intimately, but it's just a machine, doing as I command of it, all science and hard work, no magic to it. Sure, it can fail, it's only a piece or, many pieces of mechanical equipment all working together but right now, its rocking this road for me.

Most people name their bikes as if they carry the spirit of an animal or being in the same fashion, we used to name our horses. But we did not name our carriages, did we? 100 plus years ago a company might have numbered their carriages and horses to keep them organized. Naming a machine has always seemed just plain strange to me. The first story I remember about naming of a machine was that of Horatio's Drive by Ken Burns. In this awesome and very true tale of man and machine, one Horatio Nelson Jackson on a bet made in a gentleman's club, set out to drive from San Francisco to New York in his horseless carriage. The year was 1903, paved roads were as scarce and rare as gas stations back then. He purchased his horseless carriage with a gas combustion engine, hired an assistant driver, loaded up the machine with provisions and very few spare parts. He had no real mechanical experience but his wife -- had money. So, with her money and the right attitude, this young Doctor from Vermont took off across country, naming his Winton Auto Company built machine: The Vermont. This dude was a badass! He made it, but wow it took forever... like 63 days.

My favorite forward story to this 4-wheeled fame is that at the same time, a young man by the name of George Wyman was the first to ride a skoot across this country. On a California Motorbike built by Roy Marks; Wyman also started in San Francisco and got to New York faster in like 50 days. With only a pen and a writing journal, warm clothing, oil can, fuel can, camera, .357 revolver and ammo, Wyman followed mostly railroad tracks on the 90cc 1.25 horsepower motorbike. He completed the 3,700-mile journey faster than the 'Vermont' car. The answer is: the first internal combustion engine to get across this country was mounted on a skoot.

What I am personally doing out here is very American. Holding a lot of tradition in the history and people of this country. Wyman wrote all about his journey for the, then new: Motorcycle Magazine. Read it sometime if you get a chance, it's above badassery and as Americana as it gets. In keeping the moving spirit of America alive, I am out here kicking arse all over this road; here's to you George Wyman!

So, it seems the trend of naming machines started with the car and everyone jumped on the bandwagon with soft, hard, happy or evil names to describe and differentiate their cars from others, almost bringing them to life. I, like Wyman, do not do this. But wouldn't it be nice to just say 'Ole Betsy' or 'Hell Bitch' when referring to one of my many machines? It makes perfect sense for me to do this as, I was raised with a Mom who named everything, including the damn vacuum cleaner. Then there was my Pops, who seemed to shiver even thinking of referring to a machine with a human name so the answer is, numbers and strange descriptive titles will do for me, for now. This skoot is therefore the 'KZ1000 Rigid' or 'The Kawasaki Cop Rigid skoot' or 'The Police Special' or 'The Cop Moto' or 'fuck it all to hell and back!' Okay, OKAY; damn I reckon I really should just give it a name, one name and get the hell on with my life. The Problem is that I own a few of these Cop bikes, all set up differently, so numbers and code titles work best; sticking to my guns for now on this one.

These really are wonderful machines with great engineering and design. All were built the same between 1984 till 2005 so consumable parts are cheap and available. Anything that wears out or breaks can be found almost anywhere, and always in my backyard. This was the first one I owned, retired from the streets of 'The City by the Bay,' San Francisco. It's a 1989, so it has been around for a few years, proving its worth in salt and gold and has the rusty battle scars to prove it. Seeing more and doing more in its life then I could ever imagine and here it is, rebuilt and resurrected by my two hands, flying fast for me. This is a machine, my machine, and a righteous one at that. The only life it has is that which I pour into it with purchased petrol gasoline and the free air we all breath. Suck, bang, power, blow, the explosions go, propelling me forward with the twisting of my throttle hand.

Bob Marshall

Reaching down now with my left hand where my holder is mounted for my stainless-steel coffee tumbler, I pick it up. This always takes a few seconds longer out here in the wind but, I got time and it's worth it. It's a good tumbler, been with me for years and has seen many miles. As with all good things around me, it was a present from an old high school friend. Yes, it has hit the asphalt a few times showing a few good battle scars. Once it even got ran over by a Toyota truck but it's still here, serving me hot coffee. Time to lift my face shield to inhale some of this nectar of the Gods my tumbler offers up, being thankful that Ella filled it for me this morning right before the flag dropped. Coffee always tastes better when someone else serves it to me, especially when it's my hot young girlfriend. As I inhale and enjoy doing 85 m.p.h. on this smooth interstate, something starts to wiggle weird with my head. Throwing my tumbler between my legs, I grab my face shield just as it starts to fly into the wind. I managed to barely catch it on its way into traffic. With almost 3000 miles to go, a stupid new face shield is just one of those necessary evils because without it, my fair white face would suffer wind burns of biblical proportions half way through the race and, there just is not enough sun lotion or bag balm to make up for it; believe me, I have tried. The darn snaps for the face shield must have come loose – CRAP!

So now I have my coffee tumbler balanced between my knees and my face shield in my left hand. How did I not drop my tumbler onto the highway in all of this? It takes me a minute to figure it out. I can lift my left leg and jam my face shield under it. I do that. It seems to be holding so now, my coffee tumbler slowly makes its way forward to its holder after a quick stop to my lips. I pick up my left leg, find my face shield and start to tuck it in front of me, in the netting on top my headlight holding my small duffle bag. This takes a few minutes at my current speed and maneuvering of my skoot but eventually, I get it done.

No immediate remedy for this, I know I have to stop in 200 miles or so when it is time to refuel, will have to figure it out by then. Of course, I carry duct tape, hanging off the back of the skoot, ready at a moment's notice but I really need to be stopped to access it. It's right next to my lens tape, hockey stick tape and electrical tape. It's an idea.

What a great ride as the cool air kisses or slaps my face. Thankfully, Ella covered me in sun lotion before the start, and I mean like every square inch of me, my clothing only keeps so much sunlight out and I am going to be out here for a while. My fair white face should be good for a few hundred miles.

Remembering that I have my phone mounted on my handlebars, I hit the screen; turning it on and pick a social media. This of course takes me a few moments as the camera on its mount in moving around violently but, I manage to push the shutter button and kind of take a picture of myself and the brown of the Nevada desert behind me. I hit the post button, which also takes a moment. Then, comments flood back asking me where my face shield is as my face, is distorted from the wind at this speed. I laugh to myself, if I could only text a novel and race at the same time, lord knows I always have a lot to say, or write.

The Lumineers, "Ho Hey," *The Lumineers,* Dualtone, 2012.

Flying north passing by the fabulous Las Vegas, best to slow down a little and do my part to keep the fuzz away. And what do you know; there is a bit of traffic. As it stops, fellow racers are stopping with it as I simply split lanes and pass them by. Does Nevada state highway patrol have moto officers? In my rear-view mirror, I see two of my competitors start to follow my lead but within a mile, the traffic is opening. It seems Flamingo Avenue is always a popular place for lots of stop and not so much go. Moving again now, fast enough to get by, yet slow enough that I don't think law enforcement would view me as a danger to myself or those around me.

The problem is that we all kind of stick out in a crowd of cars. Our skoots look nothing like others and we draw attention wherever we go. Sometimes it is the car next to me looking out their window. Other times it's the big arse semi-trucks moving over into my lane because they are too busy staring at me and my righteous funny looking skoot to STAY IN THEIR OWN DAMN LANE. Also, there is that flash of blinding white light from a car as someone is taking my picture. My favorite of course is people who slow down in front of me because they assume I am law enforcement and they are speeding, or talking on the phone, or smoking weed, or having sex, or yeah… I've gotten to see it all in the moving vehicles around me; shame on you cagers.

There is no fairing on this cop bike but I think they see the black and white and my spotlight only to assume maybe I am part of some new pilot program for Moto officers to ride around on rigid chopped skoots to blend in for a big coolness effect. Those moto officers are way cooler than us chopper types any day of the week. Whatever the reason, it is all part of riding a skoot such as this. Got to keep my head on the swivel and my eyes are always moving. Danger is everywhere, disguised like a soccer mom's minivan.

I see other competitors passing me, just flying as I think to myself: they either started late or had to stop for fuel already. Regardless, hoping I am gaining ground in the long run as I will stop less and just keep moving forward, "Go Bob, Go". Every minute is a mile and I need to chomp up the miles to take care of the business. "Let them pass Bob," I mumble to myself, "don't take the bait, let them be the bait for law enforcement." Don't get me wrong, the Highway Patrol and other law enforcement agencies around this country have a hard job to do, better them than me, and I have the highest respect for them but sometimes; I really wish they didn't look at me and compare me to the really stupid drama television shows that have been on the boob tubes lately. Damn I think my life on 2 wheels would be easier without those fuckin stereotypes. Maybe if I wore one of those cool reflective riding suits and rode a new B.M.W. or Goldwing? Maybe someday. Those guys always look like they are having fun in comfort no matter how ridiculous they look.

The skoot is doing fine! I repeat: the skoot is doing fine! I can feel it still has plenty of power and I am growing more and more confident in all the work and hours given to its performance. Ya see it's not your average run of the mill style of chopper. It's hardly a popular looking, discovery channel, magazine cover chopper at all but it does qualify and has passed inspection for this race a few times. Popular -- chopular, this thing always gets plenty of looks and stares everywhere it goes.

I started with a totally stock 1989 Kawasaki KZ 1000 Police Moto model that I picked up a few years ago on the cheap from a kid. He wanted to get into private moto escort work but decided to sell it when he realized the carburetors were acting up and the tall boots those cool escort guys wear are like 300 bucks. I had actually originally seen the skoot a year earlier for sale from another party online and wanted to purchase it then, but that party was an arse. Then, it was a little stripped down but when I bought it, it was in full dress and ready for funeral service complete with all hard bags and flashing lights.

I was married at the time, so I had my Pops meet me up in North Los Angeles, ya know where they did a lot of filming for the famed television series about cool dudes riding around on these cop skoots? Anyways; my Pops paid the kid a thousand bucks for me. I brought the fully dressed cop skoot home in the back of my truck saying, "Look what my Pops bought for me Honey, isn't he the best"? My wife was not too happy about it as I already had 2 skoots I rode regularly and parked on the back porch. But how could she put up a fight against the bike if my Pops bought it for me? I spent the next month slowly feeding my Pops cash to pay him back. I have learned this is what Righteous Fathers do for their squirrely adult children; married or not. Isn't my Pops the best?

I quickly went to work on this poor unsuspecting Police Moto. In the world of racing, nothing is sacred. My reasoning was pretty simple for choosing this model as just about every part of this thing was bullet proof and this one had obviously been through a lot in its time on service. It seemed to have been shot at, it had some weird nicks that looked like bullet holes in the back fender that had been bonded and painted over with factory issued touch up paint; cool points earned for this machine!

When I was a kid, my Pops had a 1959 Harley Police model. His was a Pan engine turned Shovel in a truly chopped frame with a 6-inch over and out springer front end. There was no front brake as the front wheel was a tiny thing, he had a mouse trap for a clutch and long raked bars that sat on the horizon and slung back over the tank. It was all black on black with a lot of chrome. When you are just a few years old, these things stick in your head as the coolest of cool, like forever. He never rode it much as it seemed to always be in pieces in the garage. I do remember the one time I watched him jump on it, kick it to life and take off down the street as I grabbed my ears in pain. Watching this freak show of awesomeness thunder in front of me, with his arms flapping and body bouncing as the rigid frame and springer front end did it's best to throw him off. That was it, I was hooked. Damn my Pops looked cool! I knew then and there that someday, I needed to get me a machine like that.

So, I got to work on this cop skoot of mine. I ripped the front fairing with windshield off, got a monster large 9-inch headlight and built a mount for it. I also mounted a spare 3-gallon fuel cell beneath it; like a Saint Bernard Alaskan dog might carry a barrel of whisky under his neck. I found a cool cop car spotlight, the kind that mount in the pillars of a police cruiser and mounted that on the right side of the headlight where I could flip on and manipulate it with my left hand, mostly using it as a backup to my headlight and a great deer spotter. I have had a few close calls with those wonderful, majestic, and dangerous creatures that love to wander on the road. A good spotlight shining in the ditch is perfect, maybe give me a little warning. The only thing us riders fear more than big rigs and distracted drivers, are deer.

From here I cut the back of the frame off and extended the swing arm 10 inches. I built struts and lowered the rear 4 inches and built pillar posts off the back of the swing arm to meet the frame and give it all extra rigidity. When most people see the bike, they assume it to still be a cop bike without the fairing as it even has the cool rear cages remounted to protect the machine when it falls over. They either pay it no mind or, stop, scratch their heads and spend minutes looking at it. I have spent hundreds of hours building and rebuilding this poor motorcycle over the last few years including the engine. It is full of tricks and small details all to aid it in this race and to get it going down the road as fast as possible, for many days at a time. For me it's perfect, just as I set it up to be.

It just doesn't take a rocket scientist to figure out that most humans like a lot of shiny, well painted, chromed out and good-looking stuff on their rides; all known as our romantic side. It all attracts the eye and turns heads. When the rider mounts it, it makes them feel good to be seen on such a well-manicured, head turning machine of folkloric wonder and amazement to the common man. They might even give these awesomely built machines names, or characters all to aid in the self-purpose of what the machines serves them for, why they have it, or built it, or had it built. My skoot, is nothing like that. Oh, sure all the parts I have made or remade have a good few coats of rattle can primer and black paint on them but, there is no show chrome on this machine. Any of the chrome is original and faded from the years of service the bike endured in the lovely salt air of that seaside city. I know it's from San Fran because it still has their Barcode sticker on the frame under the seat. I assume this sticker was part of a scanning system the city used -- to know what Moto it was exactly when it came in for service. They would scan it and pop up all this information they needed on the Moto on their commodore 64 or whatever beast of a word processor they had in their City Moto Repair Shop in 1989.

With the spare fuel cell and original tank, I carry about 7 gallons, good for about 220, maybe 250 miles before I have to hit the reserve lever. So yeah, between 30 and 40 miles to the gallon depending on how hard I twist my ole' throttle hand. Luckily it has a huge reserve, maybe 50 miles before we just run completely out of fuel and stop. Sometimes I hit the reserve around 180 miles and sometimes 240; just depends on the road, weather, and how much lead I got in my throttle hand. All of this, in my opinion, is the 'make or break' of the race. I like to pick my fuel stops as carefully as possible. Stopping on the right side of the highway is best to avoid left turns or waiting for old traffic lights or old motorhomes and their occupants at old stop signs. I prefer the higher priced gas stop as it should be less crowded and blah blah this is a race; I really don't care about saving a few cents on fuel prices.

Scanning the horizon now, it's time to find one. There it is. It looks open and ready for my business, off to the right, just past one of those bargain gas stations. I have not hit the reserve yet on my main tank, but I am sure it's been over 200 miles since the start so it's near time, and this station, is perfect.

Robbie Robertson and The Band, "The Weight." Capitol Records, 1968.

Riding the last 50 miles or so next to me on his raked out chop we call the 'Deer Slayer,' is my competitor and good friend Velarde Gonzalez. He has hit 2 deer with this righteous machine and managed to plow through a small compact car that pulled out in front of him on his way to the starting line this morning. Velarde is a well-built man and shows no sign of his early thirties age. He usually wears button down shirts if he is wearing a shirt at all; with cool patterns and good worn jeans held up by true leather suspenders, attaching his holster for his firearm. His boots are just as you would expect, equally well-worn and colorful. He always removes his hat when meeting a lady, tells you his full name and shakes hands very well. I speak so highly of him as he has gotten me and many, I know out of a tough spot a time or two. He is covered in his newly purchased rain gear as everyone but me seemed certain it would rain this morning.

I point to my tank and wave off to him and a few others behind us in our custom 'stupidly over excited' racers wave. I wish I knew how to describe this wave we came up with years ago, it is the most ridiculous, over exaggerated hand gesture imaginable on a skoot. If you were driving your car near us, I suspect the only thing that gets you more alert than a ragtag bunch of scary looking dudes on choppers is; a ragtag bunch of scary looking dudes on choppers with shit eating grins waving to each other like a bunch of excited little girls. Humor is a wonderful spice to life, much needed in this form of badassery. He leans over giving me a good fist bump as I slow my skoot for the off ramp.

#4

Pulling off to refuel; this is where the real race begins and ends. An 8-minute fuel stop would be preferred, of course it could probably be done in 3 minutes if I didn't have to use the restroom, refill my coffee, get water or food, etc... I could just piss on the pump and drink the rain. I suspect some of the first-place finishers do this, but I really like my coffee, water and snacks and yeah, bathroom breaks.

Snuffing out my smoke in my ashtray that's strapped to my handlebars with hockey stick tape and making 2 right turns, I find the petrol station. Oh, how so many years ago every young man dreamed of hitting the highway on their righteous over built monster Harley, seeing America like they had never seen it before and visiting every petrol station along the way. The peanut tanks of the classic chops were just not big enough to hold much fuel, bouncing from station to station is just what they did, hence; my spare fuel cell sitting under my headlight with an extra 3 gallons of ozone depleting, throttle twisting power.

Finding a roll in/roll out pump where I can see the skoot from inside the store can be a challenge, but I manage it here. This won't always be my plan of attack but for now, leaving the skoot at the pump for a few minutes while I run inside is my preference. No person too shady seem to be around unless you count me, and one of my competitors. His tool pouch is out, and something is taken apart as he sits butt down on the ground, concentrated and hard at it. Don't know him personally but I had met him and his red beard at the starting line and I got to eye up his awesome machine. He has done some good work on it; an early 1980's Suzuki J engine or inline 4 in a stellar classic and tall raked out frame, with a lot of chrome and lack of paint. Damn I must work harder on remembering people by name. I can shake their hand, say their name back to them and still I have issue remembering. My Pops with all his professional business sense and accomplishment would be disappointed in me right about now. This man's name was Caleb I recalled later, but at this time, I could not remember that to save my life. Maybe I just have a few other things on my mind...

With a wave and good morning again as I walk by, he starts talking to me. "Yeah I think I got the hosa thingy stuck in the…"

I interrupt him, "Are you going to be able to fix it and keep moving? Do you need anything?"

"Oh yeah" he replies with a big smile on his face, "I got it."

"Cool!" I reply. "Well it's a beautiful day, get back out there asap and enjoy your road Amigo!"

Time to enter the store, walking with purpose as usual. Hope Caleb did not think me too rude; this is a race and neither of us have time to chat about skoots. If he has got it all figured out, I will catch up with him at the end of the race over coffee or beer and hear his story then. No time for those 'stop and chats' now, I'm way too hyper of a human to be polite sometimes and now, is definitely one of those times.

Go Bob Go! Hitting the bathroom; stowing the coffee tumbler in the back pocket of my oversized overalls, I pony up to the urinal, unzip, pee and stretch out my upper body. I feel good right now and don't really need the stretch as it's only been a few hours of riding. This is just a good habit I've gotten into over the years, stretch a little while peeing. I can feel the cool on my legs as they are almost numb by now from the cool morning ride with only my overalls, but it will warm up soon out here in this desert. Most people are going to church or big buffet breakfasts, maybe sleeping off some alcoholic coma from last night right about now across these United States of America and here I am, in my own sanctuary, on the road. Here on my skoot moving forward on this beautiful interstate built for and by the taxpayers. Fresh air in my face and the road moving just a few inches beneath my feet on my machine, damn how I love to run on this road.

With two shakes and a flush, I am hitting the sink. No soap… whatever, no time for common things like hygiene. Exiting the bathroom and filling my tumbler with half of the dark roast and half house coffee blend. I like the extra caffeine of the dark but don't need it giving me heartburn out here as it sometimes can. A shot or 2 of creamer and I grab a stick of jerky for later, teriyaki, not spicy pepper, again the less heartburn the better. I'm almost 40 years old, the spices have become a little hard on my stomach if I do not manage it correctly. No line at the counter, score! Nothing slows my racing mojo down like a line of slow, card swiping individuals. Hitting the attendant with a few bills from my wallet then walking outside past my competitor. Yeah, I'm going to have to remember to hear Caleb's story at the finish line, for sure he will have some good ones with all the excitement of a younger man in this cross-country chopper race.

I slide my card in the pump and stretch my hips. I hope to do this instinctually in the next few days to keep my legs working. Unlock my fuel tanks and start refilling with that golden petrol fuel, smiling and happy to be out of California and away from those foreskin nozzles that have to be held back manually. This is a bit of a dance for me and the weak point on my set up on this machine but, over the years I have learned to embrace this dance as good exercise. Filling my main tank with premium -- just under 3 gallons. I then let the pump handle sit on the seat while walking around to the other side of the bike, undo the net on the front holding my small duffle bag where the filler of the other fuel cell is located. Unscrew the cap, hold the bars straight so they don't flop over as the bike is leaned to the left on its kickstand. I grab the pump nozzle, put it in and pull the handle to fill. Paying close attention to how it's filling without losing concentration of what's around me is always tricky business. I suspect this is when I'd get whacked in the back of the head and robbed. All my senses are alert right now, but I've learned that kind of stuff really doesn't happen. The road is just not that dangerous, no matter how much the television set tell us it is. Just over 2 gallons in this tank, it holds almost 3 so it still had a little fuel left in it. That's a good thing, my estimating skills seem to be okay as I figured it was a little premature stopping now and my figuring, was correct.

My G.P.S. is not working correctly, damn -- this is going to be a long trip. Well, that's what I get for thinking technology would take care of me or be able to operate on a skoot such as mine. The whole rigid frame, bumping and bouncing everywhere thing. This G.P.S. is a few years old and not a common model but big enough that I can see it well. However, it keeps going to fuzzy white screen, has shut itself off twice, and gotten way lost. I will need to work more on good old instinct to find my gas stations and know my mileage. Oh well, guess it can be a good thing as it's one more thought to be calculated in my head, keeping my mind sharp and focused.

Now I get to perform the reverse of all I just did and grab the pump receipt, stowing it in a plastic baggy I have tucked in the inside pocket of my riding vest. All receipts for this race are required as proof I stayed on the designated route. This keeps people from riding 100 miles then throwing their skoot in the back of a box trailer while their team of people take turns driving cross country as fast as possible only to unload 100 miles from the finish line. I am not sure if anyone has ever really tried that and don't think it would work as it takes time to fuel a vehicle and the whole loading and unloading of the bike thing, also takes time. To keep questions and conspiracy theories from arising, we simply keep the receipts as they are timed, dated, and location stamped.

About now, competitor Caleb is jumping on and firing up his skoot. He rides over to me, "We'll see ya down the road." I nod, give him a thumbs up as he waves and smiles, jamming gears as he pulls away. Time for me to get my giddy on as well. Buttoning up my riding vest making sure my earbud wires are straight where they should be. I have gotten in the habit of undoing my vest anytime I am not directly riding on the skoot or just taking it off stowing it under a bungee net on the back of the skoot. After all; it is a riding vest, not a 'hanging out in' vest. With all the extra stuff I carry, it can be odd to wear while not riding as its heavy, leather and full of everything I need to survive for a month in the wilderness or a zombie apocalypse. I have stuffed some weird stuff in this poor vest throughout the years and have gotten so used to it, it would be hard to ride without it. And it's all set on right or left side, inside or outside pockets depending on the item.

In the clutch hand or left outer pocket, there is usually an assortment of small candies: Lifesaver mints in peppermint and spearmint, both regular and sugar free, hard and soft caramel candies, and just about anything else that's hard and will not melt too easily. Above all, my coffee candies. Oh, how I love my coffee candies on a good long ride, just a nice steady stream of caffeine to aid my body and mind. Yup, I'm a junkie, I LOVE the stimulating effects of caffeine via almost any form of consumption. In my left front watch pocket rides my mp3 player. The earbud cord runs under the vest then up the inside tucking under my neckerchief or big bandana worn around my neck and up to my ears. On my right I hold my smokes and a lighter sometimes on the outside pocket along with an extra mp3 player, that has a little different music so I can change them up as the mood strikes me, but they are virtually the same model. In the front right, a great bundle of AAA batteries taped together for easy access and quick replacement while flying down the road for these mp3 players. The inside pockets are, of course, not accessible at 80 miles an hour so I keep my small sandwich bags of receipts, my small tube of sunscreen, a sharpie for my friends to use in signing autographs for all the adoring fans while attending chopper shows, a pile of my stickers and my rosary. It all equals a kind of the glove box or center console of my riding world. We as humans have all gotten very used to having all our 'stuff' close at hand, I simply wear it all in my vest.

Under all of this and my shirt I keep a set of dog tags, with all my emergency info: my religion, an emergency phone number of a friend, my allergies and above all, the fact that I am not a donor. Please try to save me in the event of an accident and do not harvest this beat up body of mine for organs, thank you. I also have a dog tag made by F Bomb just for this race. It has a Stampede 10 embossed on one side and on the other, an outline of the U.S.A. Wow, what a token, and Uncle Bomb was even kind enough to make some extras; giving one to my son. Oh, the joy in that young man's eyes when he received that bit of awesomeness.

Assessing my face shield situation, I pull some duct tape from my roll that's hanging off the back side of the skoot. I can see I have scratched it and the scratches are deep and, going to cause me a huge visual issue on this ride; well, it is what it is, and all part of the adventure. Maybe the distraction will keep me awake, I gotta look at the positive here dammit! I could find somewhere to stop and get another one, but I don't have time for that and even if I did, I don't want to take the time for that. Fuck it, duct tape will have to do, and the scratches are just character, Stampede Approved.

I rebutton and attach it to the 3-button setup on the top front of my ¾ helmet, taping it as I see fit. Red duct tape is what I happened to bring and now it is everywhere on the front top of my helmet. I also noticed it was rubbing my chin when in the down position, so I add a piece of tape there as well. That would be a bloody mess if that rubbed through my chin and my beard is already red, yeah that could hurt. This whole face shield thing is just not my normal M.O. but it's going to keep me going without wearing down my face so a necessary evil it is. I strap my helmet on and slip on my gloves. Kicking up the kickstand while grabbing a handful of clutch, I hit the start button and motor away.

Rob Zombie, "Never Gonna Stop" *The Sinister Urge* Geffen Records, 2009.

Back on the interstate now, I start to wonder how my new Girlfriend Ella is doing. She had seen me off on this adventure at the starting line. My motley crew of a family and a group of friends came out to see all of us off this morning - always a good compliment. Even my friend Jake Krotje 'The Flying Dutchman' drove in from Las Vegas late last night and slept in his car at the gas station next to the hotel to witness the start of this mayhem. If you don't know who Jake is, look him up some time, the man is a crazy metalworking artistic badass who always manages to inspire with all he creates and builds. I heard something about them all going to breakfast after I took off. Naturally I would like to stop and text Ella or call but I really do not have that option while moving and shaking out here on the road. I start looking at my phone mounted on the handlebars and open it, nothing. I will trust, as always, that no news, is good news.

I did get a message from my mistress wishing me luck and good fortune. Wow, how I miss that woman. I have not seen her for several days which is not like us, but I have been so busy lately with my skoot and my new girlfriend that I just have not had a minute to hear her voice. Yeah, she has that voice. It is so young, so smooth and her infectious tones just hit my ears like the timbre of strings on a well-tuned mandolin. All notes working deep into the naughty parts of my brain and body. Our physical and sexual relationship has always been at our convenience and totally absent lately but, going several days without hearing her voice is wearing on me. Her message to me simply reads; "Hi Daddy! I see by now you are off and running in your race. Good luck and have an amazing time. I can't wait to hear all the stories you bring back. So, as you like to say, 'Go fast, go straight'. Oh, and your new girlfriend is still a CUNT! Come back to me in one-piece Daddy, I will be here waiting for you!"

Yeah; that woman really knows how to get to me alright, I also know that she knows this and does it on purpose, making my cock rock hard with just a few simple words. How I wish her place in life and mine were on a similar path, but we all know these kinds of statements can lead to trouble, just self-inflicted, downward spiraling, kick yourself in the nuts, trouble. Terms like "I wish" are not usually in my vocabulary. I have learned the hard way to not fight someone and, I just refuse to fight her for her. It would be nice if she thought higher of Ella but, I will simply have to view her opinion as healthy jealousy and take it as a compliment. They had met once in a social setting, I know she was hoping they would get along wonderfully and a few hot sexual threesomes would ensue but; when they did meet, it was not the fireworks show she was hoping for. Bummer for all of us and I have learned to not force these types of things. Good things always happen for those who wait. So maybe next time, as they say. My mistress is a very smart and educated woman with a lot under her surface. I have learned to trust her and her intuition on everything. She seems to see things before they happen and has reaction skills above and beyond that of an average human. Damn I like this mistress of mine but it sure would be nice if she had a higher opinion of Ella. Maybe she sees something I don't? Damn, I'm gonna have to think on that one and figure something out, eventually.

The relationship my mistress and I share is built on friendship and admiration for our sexual play. She served me in an extremely submissive fashion as I served her in a very opposite, Dominant style. I am simply THE man who was fortunate enough to fulfill her wildest sexual fantasies no matter how taboo they may be for the human race. It's just one of those things you are either born with it or not. Some people are all into it or shrug it off, while some run from it. In my life I have been fortunate enough to indulge in these taboos of sexual lifestyle and enjoy them. These days, I simply embrace it and live it, even with Ella. Of course, in a similar yet unique fashion as relationships are all very unique with this lifestyle and no two are alike.

It had occurred to me just recently how most men seem to just think, or ponder, or simply dream of things. Maybe they have a monthly magazine subscription or a favorite program on the television but for the most part, it seems they just dream of it. My character seems to always just jump into things so here I am, racing and road running with wonderful sexually serving women on my mind.

I need to figure out how to lose the tall admiration I have for my mistress. The simple answer is she left her husband for some time and recently, decided to move back in with him and work things out. She is not my mistress as I am, by social definition, her Mister. A term I prefer not to be involved in so several months ago when she figured out that she wanted to be with her husband again, we stopped our play time and since, have simply remained friends. We are both very proud of this in this situation and often laugh with each other about it as most would have had issue by now but, here we are friends, and damn I enjoy her friendship, maybe a little too much so yeah, going to have to tune that part of my brain, and tune it well.

Allman Brothers, "One Way Out." *Eat a Peach,* Capricorn Records, 1972.

Just what I need to hear right about now.

American Road Runner

#5

Back to the road now, accelerating through the gears with some well-deserved music filling my ears. All those human noises and that commercialization at the gas stations can really bug my inner self sometimes. It seems people make noise just to hear themselves. I reckon I am not excluded from doing this, but all the machines, air conditioning, freezers, lights, all humming at different frequencies and timbres with none relating to each other. Damn all that can really bug the shit out of me -- if I let it. Then the darn gas pumps try to talk to you with a screen, yeah screw that crap, that's just dangerously distracting. Combined it all makes for a symphony of a mind numbing, brainwave interrupting mess. I can only stand it for so long then I have to get back on the road, back to my Zen.

I've been listening to The Allman Brothers and other great rock music since I was in my Mom's tummy. My Pops used to share the records with me via headphones, the same set of headphones that I still have and rebuild several years back. Using them all through my younger years and college days until my teenage daughter procured them from me, appropriately, as all of our children seem to do with our stuff. I'm glad she is enjoying them, they are the real, big comfy, old school 'realistic' deal. At the end of the day you either have kids or you have stuff, I like my kids, they can have my stuff.

Heading northeast, somewhere near a township park called Moaba it seems. I reckon most would stop and figure out exactly where they are, but I just don't have the time for that right now. A little sad, but all part of this road race. Time to simply enjoy the beauty of it all from this interstate. The route I am traveling will eventually lead me to other roads then, to the other side of the country, at least that's the plan on the map, and I am hoping to make it there in one piece.

Motley Crue, "Wildside." *Girls, Girls, Girls,* Elektra Records, 1987

We were giving the set route at 6 p.m. last night, copied on an 8 ½ by 11 sheet of paper. It was a picture of the United States with a black line drawn on the route and a few written navigational instructions in the margins, some legible, some not so much. That's half the fun, doing my best to figure out the written route without the wave points or pinpoints or whatever they may be called on a fancy G.P.S. unit.

This guy named Nomad Charlie writes and squiggles all over this map to give direction. Yeah, I hate that guy, and he hates me back. He hates all of us competitor types. He is just set to torture us with this race we call the Stampede. Charlie is the guy who puts the race map together for us, inspects our chopped skoots and collects our money for distribution later. Without him, this little hop across the country would not exist. He also writes about it in a chopper magazine called The Horse Backstreet Choppers, glorifying it for all it is worth and forcing people like me to fall in love with it. Most of this is his fault, without his writings, I would surely not be here. I'd most likely be home, watching T.V. that is if I had T.V. and just dreaming of riding my skoot to places and not, actually racing. Damn this

Charlie guy knows how to write and, race. For several years he has come in first or second. His smaller well-built frame astride one of his many righteous chops and his 'not give a fuck about much' attitude usually gets him the trophy. Yeah okay, I have a lot of admiration for this guy, this race and our lifestyle of riding all over this country. I have also had the luxury of becoming good friends with him and his Ole' Lady Jill. They are also good friends with F Bomb and have known him a lot longer than I have. They all live near each other around Phoenix Arizona. So yeah, we all kind of get to know each other and share in each other's passion for building, riding and racing, until the flag drops, then it's all business and every competitor for themselves.

I have this paper map in my clear map holder on the top of my tank bag, between my legs. I won't really need it till the end where the race jumps around on a few smaller or blue highways, trying to figure out exactly what Charlie wrote to get to the finish line but in the meantime, it's nice to have it staring back at me in my peripheral vision as a reminder why I am out here. I will use this time to memorize the last of the route. Then when it's time to travel said route, I can just do so as it is doubtful my eyes or brain will be working correctly by then. Keeping most of it covered up with a foldable road map of the country, I don't need anybody seeing the route map paper especially, law enforcement and figuring out myself or any of my competitors are doing what we are doing. Competing in an illegal and totally unsanctioned cross country skoot race; that would be bad, for all of us. As far as anyone knows, the Stampede does not exist! I am not racing or competing in anything! This is a rule we all get to adhere too with strict religious conviction to keep law enforcement from giving us any heat. I will eat the damn map if I have too to keep it out of sight of the wrong eyes. The Stampede, this race across this wonderful country on beaten up old chopped skoots does not exist!

Some quick math, the answer was twelve-minute refuel at the last stop. I will have to do better and get a little faster in the very near future, for now let's blame my face shield failure on the slow stop. I know small inconveniences like that are going to happen, I plan for them and carry a lot of tools, spare parts, duct tape, hockey stick tape, safety wire and other cool shit in preparation. Repairs both big and small just take time and I will have to make good judgement calls when they happen like; if I want to even repair them or just go without, whatever they may be, only time will tell.

Damn this is some pretty country, starting to wonder if I'll get to see any purple sage on the road ahead this time of year? I think it would be many miles ahead in the middle and northern parts of Utah maybe, I just can't seem to remember right now. Crap I wish I knew; my Pops would know the answer to this. Could try to Google it but, yeah not at this speed or in this kind of turbulence. My phone mounted to my handlebars in front of me is kind of freaking out right now. All the vibrations of the rigid ride are making it go a little... haywire. Will have to leave the screen shut off and just check it periodically to see if I have missed anything important or, I could just ignore the fucker all together! Humm, that's a good idea but a hard one to wrap my spoiled American brain around.

I have great memories of being in this part of the country as a young boy with my Pops, sitting in the passenger seat of one of his big Caprice Classic Station Wagon company cars and asking what all those purple colored bushes were on the side of the road? He reached in the back seat like a Dad does. Usually it was to hand out a spanking to myself and my siblings but this time; with a happy look on his face, he handed me a paperback book, "here, read".

An old worn-down novel graced my hands and eyes, a book by someone called Zane Grey, "Riders of the Purple Sage". I started to read and kind-of got sick with how much the word 'gentile' appeared but, slowly I made my way through the first chapter - with a thousand questions for my Pops. It did not take me long to learn and know that other worlds are out there, all there for the taken by me, and those worlds are in books. My Pops consumes several books a month, now I got to really understand why. Being back here in this land, reminding me of all those great road trips my Pops and I got to experience together is quite the treat. It all reminds me that anything is possible in my small life, even writing this book that you are reading now.

Where the Nevada desert kisses the north west corner of Arizona and into the south west corner of Utah, the monuments start rising and the color changes to that pretty tan red that artists strive to recreate in landscapes. They get pretty darn close but being in this scene, on this land, reminds me that these colors and rock formations are truly awesome and can only be made by our universe on this beautiful planet. Being on my skoot, running up this road, being part of this scene is just pure livin' for me, L-I-V-I-N, and just what the doctor ordered. Damn I could spend all day and night running up and down this stretch of road, never tiring or wanting for much more out of life.

Back to the business at hand; I have full tanks of fuel and about 250 miles between needed fuel stops. Sure, better gas mileage is available if, slower speeds are obtained, but yeah, that's not in the cards for me right now so fuck that shit. I will be cutting that mileage a little short in hopes of NOT running dry as sitting on the side of the road without fuel will really eats up precious minutes. However, I know stopping too often will eat up the same precious minutes so this must be managed and well. Not having a speedometer or trip gauge on this skoot to aid me in this, I did manage to bring a G.P.S. but, yeah... it never gave me this kind of issue before. I guess if I were a small electronic device mounted to a rigid machine going this fast, I would cut out and lose power also. The big reason I brought along the G.P.S. is to scroll out and see what's in front of me and around me in hopes of being able to find a good gas station when needed. This is a game of skill, science, and sometimes just dumb luck. Whether I need just fuel or fuel, coffee and a pee break with maybe a side of beef jerky and trail mix will really be the deciding factors on where to stop. Of course, crowds, those damn crowds, play a big part in this as well. If a gas station is crowded with kids and cagers all standing around waiting for something to entertain them, well let's just say that scene is to be avoided. By cagers I mean, people who drive cars, and the cages that they are. I would rather starve and go without then deal with lines to the restroom and comments about the foreign but needed attire I adorn. Damn, it would be good to see what's around me with a G.P.S., especially at night. Mostly I would love to see my elevation and if there are mountains around in hopes of being prepared or not surprised by bad weather, or worse, deer. Aw yes, lovable cuddle deer that grace our American roadways. So beautiful, and my worst nightmare here on the road. If I can see mountains and hills around me, the deer might be there, luckily the highway departments occasionally put up signage. Yeah, very few things make me sit forward and pay attention like a deer crossing sign. Personally, I have not hit a deer or fallen asleep but have come pretty darn close. I have heard horror stories from friends like; that time F Bomb was riding back in the state of New York at night with a buddy in staggered formation. A big north country deer ran across the road, in- between them. Wow! Stories like that that remind me how much the universe has blessed me.

Wonder how F Bomb is doing? Well, and my other competitors for that matter? I suspect Bomb is a few miles behind me now, moving slower, but well, in this beautifully cool and calm weather. No news is good news so, I won't be worrying too much about him as he is a grown arse man and has gotten this far in life. He also has a lot more experience, dedication and sacrifice to this race than any of us out here running it today. He will be fine; I will see him at the finish line.

The scariest encounter with our four-legged enemy is from Valarde Gonzalez, as I mentioned earlier. He has hit 2 deer on his laid-back chopper we now dub 'Deer Slayer,' hitting one and getting the bike off the ground and then a year or so later ramming through another one; always busting himself up a little but he keeps going. Maybe it's the long girder front end or the high center point of his frame, or maybe, he is just blessed. I am not sure of all the dates and times and circumstances as Valarde is definitely that type of quiet man who does not like to boast. He has hurt himself during these incidents but will keep quiet about it as he would hate for anyone to worry about him. And yeah, he has also cut through a car and a tree as well; that we know of.

The engine on this Cop Chop of mine has not had any sort of issue in the last few hundred miles since I rebuilt it and that, is promising to me right now and assists in lowering my anxiety levels. A few years back in this race on this machine, we were riding highway 10 from west to east and somewhere in the middle of Texas, I started losing a ton of power. On top of that; at the Louisiana border I hit a torrential rainstorm that brought blinding sheets of water right to my face shield and neck.

Breathing was hard with all the water shedding off my face shield at speed and slamming my precious windpipe. I pulled off the road, figuring ripping my carbs apart and trying to figure what the hell is going on would be a much more productive use of my time than trying to move forward. So, there I am; in a rainstorm, in the parking lot of a motel where I got a room, under the handy 2-dollar tarp I always carry, ripping my carbs off my machine and then apart in the motel room. I found nothing obviously wrong or out of place so I put them back on, took a few hours' worth of a nap, a shower, and continued on for more than a thousand miles at 4 thousand rpm's in 4th gear, which equaled about 50 miles an hour on a flat road. Just for reference, most highways across this country have a 65 or 75 m.p.h. speed limit. And, by the way, humidity from a rainstorm, really keeps the smell of gas hanging in a motel room. No amounts of fans or open windows and doors could of getting rid of that petrol smell in that poor room, good thing I paid cash without a receipt. Moving slowly as I was, everyone's Mother, Grandmother and even a few street sweepers passed me but, eventually after a lot of patience and learning to ride while watching my rear view mirror, I finished the race in Rockingham, North Carolina, 16th place out of 40 some odd competitors that year, in about 3 ½ days. Good lesson that moving well and fast involves more on the moving well side. Ya gotta keep going sometimes and eventually, you will get it done even, if that's 16th place.

    Right after that ordeal I rested for a few days and enjoyed the festivities of the chopper show there known as "The Smoke Out". I just had to use some starting fluid to get the bike running again after it sat for more than an hour and cooled. Luckily, my friend Nomad Charlie had a can to loan me; forever.

    The next Monday after the weekend festivities, I jumped on a plane to get west and back home to the family in California and had the bike shipped back to me. I left it at a dealership in Charlotte, North Carolina who charged me nothing to park it there for a week till the bike shipping company showed up to bring it back to me. Yes, there are shipping companies who use cool old Nascar double decker trailers to pick up and drop off skoots all over the country. Give them a few weeks and they can get your bike anywhere. Scary how many people do not ride their bikes around but have them shipped. For me it was simply the last resort just short of selling the machine on the east coast for parts. It was a pricey service but after all this skoot and I had been through, I was okay giving it a little love, shipping it back to myself and keeping it.

I have to admit the driver of this awesome bike shipping rig was a pretty righteous dude. He had to meet me in a church parking lot around the block from my house as I live on a smaller dead-end street. When I walked around the corner with my then 5-year-old son in tow, the driver was all smiles in telling me how he picked my bike up in Detroit and, naturally had a few good questions about its purpose. There it was, all beat up and dirty amongst a big arse trailer full of shiny Harleys. He explained that he had to lower my bars to get it to fit correctly on the bottom level of the trailer. On top of this he noticed I had left my coffee tumbler in its holder and took the liberty to wash out the old, creamer filled coffee. Apparently, my famed tumbler had developed a smell. I had to laugh and thank him profusely while tipping him accordingly.

My son and I pushed the skoot around the block and back to the home laboratory. Okay I pushed, my son just kind of rode on it. We made quick work of it getting it up on the bench. Now when I say bench, I mean my standard looking workbench I made out of 2x4s and some plywood. It's 2 feet wide, 7 feet long, and about 20 inches tall. I put a ramp on one side, push the skoot up on it in the middle of my little carriage shed of a garage and can sit in my chair and wrench away as needed.

I hit the cylinders of my poor beaten engine with my compression tester and as I suspected I had lost a ton of compression which equaled losing a ton of power. Out of 4 cylinders, there was full compression in number 1, half compression in number 2 and zero compression in cylinders 3 and 4. This wonderful 1000 cubic centimeter cop engine had killed itself pushing me across country, very admirably. I was sold from then on that my love affair with these engines, and specifically this one, was going to last a very, very long time.

I made quick work of ripping the top of the engine apart, ordered some oversized pistons and rings and had the cylinder jugs bored out accordingly to accommodate them. Then I had the same machinist do a valve job for me, I mean heck, why not splurge and let a true professional get it as right as right could be, right? I blue printed the engine and totally immersed myself in all the cool details to keep this engine going for me. It's like arts and crafts with oil and a lot of measuring and re-measuring of cool metal parts that work together to keep the engine sucking, banging, powering and blowing. I put it all back together and fired it up. It ran, but seemed a little, off. Taking it for a test ride, I got a few miles down the road and one of the valves really started knocking followed by a ping sound, followed by a grinding sound. Holy heck; I must of done something very wrong and really messed something up,,,crap! I had to stop the bike and push it the few blocks home.

Putting the poor skoot back on the bench, I tore my recently completed work apart, again. As I pulled the valve cover, or H cover as it is sometimes called on these models of engines because it looks like the letter H, it showed me very quickly what had gone wrong. One of the top intake cam half bearings had fallen out of place and went straight for the transmission, exploding shrapnel all over the place. "This has to be your DAMN fault Bob!" I had to rip the bottom of the engine apart, crawl under it and really clean all these very small pieces of bearing from every nook and cranny of the engine and transmission, they are one of the same on this machine. I also pulled the head to check the valves as one of the plugs showed me, somehow, it had some oil in it already. One can tell a lot of what's going on inside the internal combustion of an engine from the spark plugs. Mostly checking spark plugs can tell ya how the carburetors are running but, to already have some black from some oil, that made no sense. One of the valves was already bent and scratched. I pulled it off and realized the guide was broken, an entire piece of the guide was missing and nowhere to be found. If it had broken off, lately, the broken piece would have sat there in the spring under the grommet but that was not the case.

The damn machining company that was hard to find in the first place in the next town over of San Bernardino had broken it and put it back together anyways. I was terribly disappointed, and it reassured me that I just need to do all my work myself that way when something goes wrong I know exactly who to blame. I make this statement so bold in life lately as I have learned the same to be true, it all has to begin and end with me, in all aspects of my life. I am responsible for me, and all that happens to me and all I do for me and mine.

So here I am, in the middle of the open road: roaring fast and loud with an engine that I rebuilt myself, on a bike I rebuild myself and it leaves me in awe that it is working so well. I feel totally in tuned with it, this, my machine, my stuff. It just wants to go and go and take me with it.

Toto, "Africa," *Toto IV*, Columbia Records, 1982.

We all know that, as a society we have turned from doers and shakers of our own worlds to - debt ridden consumers that just…well…consume, no matter what the cost sometimes. The motorcycle industry is no different and has suffered in some respects while thriving in others because of this. Today you can hit the showroom floor, sling down a good job and credit rating and get all you need to look like that Americana folklore idea of a: 'born to be wild' biker. You get the jacket, the boots, the big black motorcycle and, you can add all the bolt on parts your credit card can handle to "customize" your machine and make it unique, like everyone else is doing around you on the showroom floor. Every Saturday morning you dress up, saddle up and cruise 11.2 miles to your favorite breakfast joint with some fellow bikers for your favorite chicken fried steak and eggs meal. Don't get me wrong, I am always happy to see men and women out enjoying recreation and damn I love a good chicken fried steak, OBVIOUSLY, but this is not what my life is about nor is it truly what skootin' on a skoot is about, in my humble opinion. I don't have a warranty on my skoot, hell I don't even have an auto club subscription or a towing service. I have me, and my skill. Sometimes this includes tens of hours of concentration and maybe a little frustration to figure out a problem, but I am totally in tune with my stuff, my machine. I have taken it all apart and put it all back together, sometimes more than once to get it right. I spend my money on good parts, not cheap chrome bolt on accessories. This is my passion for how I enjoy my life and the cool stuff in my life like my old home, or the mechanical workings of my home, or my trucks, my skoots, it's all the same.

I work smart, not hard and have a good time finding the problems and working them out to resolve a solution that works for me and my stuff. It is a great relationship I like to set up and nurture. This is just me; no better, no worse than the next man who lives preferring to owe for what he has rather then get too involved in it or pay cash.

My Pops is big on this always reminding me that "You can't beat a man at his own game Son". Thanks Pops but watch me compete! Although, it has to be added that my Pops IS the laziest man I know and will always stop, look at a problem, find the easiest solution and get it done faster than the next guy, and yes; that including me. I said he was lazy, not a bum. I can go on and on about this subject but it's better if I simply recommend the writings of Matthew Crawford in his book, 'Shop Class as Soulcraft.' Read it, know it, live and love yourself and your stuff more from it.

At the end of the day I am so thankful for the community of riders we have in this country. Without them, I would not be able to do what I do. Rather it be the trickle-down effect of cost on the used machines I purchased or, the respect I get from most people driving with me on this road. It seems everyone out here in a cage probably has a loved one who rides even if it's just on the weekends. I owe a lot to everyone who rides, no matter what they ride or how they ride and yes, this includes pedal bicycles, trikes and sidecars, tot goats, whatever.

It always amazes me how quick this highway goes from big wide brown desert to a 2 laner with a little green here and there. I have gotten out of California a while back and that always makes me feel good but always a little, well, indifferent. I may still be in a desert, but no longer in my familiar California Desert. I was born and raised in Southern California, Riverside to be exact. The Inland Empire they call it, and still own my little house there across the street from the home my parents owned when I was born. I was able to purchase my current home in my early 20's from my family. It's always been a family home as far as I know. Hell, most of the neighbors still call me Bobby. They think of me as a little dude racing my BMX bikes up and down the street. I still do that, only now my bikes have engines and make a little more noise. Usually the neighbors peek out their front doors to see what I'm riding or what I may of rebuilt that day. I guess I just don't know any better or different or want for anything else. I have a good job with the County there as a Building Mechanic where I get to fix things all day long for my fellow Riverside County Employees. Mostly locksmith and door type of tasks are assigned to me, but nothing is beneath me and every day is different. Pay is good, the benefits are good, my Boss is awesome, and I get time off to do squirrely shit like this.

My background is a little rougher than most. I always thrived and worked hard for all the traditional important things in life sold to us on what we like to call 'The American Dream'. So, way back when I was a young man, I met a wonderful woman in my early 20s, courted her in the current typical fashion, and then she said "Yes". We had the most wonderful wedding, the best I had ever attended anyways, however like most things, it was not meant to be forever. She got to a point where she no longer wanted to be married to me. After much debate, pleading and eventually acceptance, I had to let her go, granting her the divorce she wanted without question just a few years ago. Today I am a single Dad dating a much younger woman and racing my skoot across country. Wow, life can change so quickly in such a short period of time, no matter what you plan for.

Little Feat, "Willin," *Little Feat,* Warner Bros. Records, 1971.

Maybe the Mormons were on to something up here in this red desert. How fortunate I feel to live in this place and time, to have these roads to move on and fuel to burn. Passing big rigs on my right with only the occasional lead footer in a hopped-up sports car or some type of small compact family car. Let them pass me; they will wave off any law enforcement ahead that might view my excess of speed as an issue. I am a true believer that if ya go just a little above the speed of those around you, it keeps all your attention up front, and it all equals less distraction.

No need to over worry about what's behind you or even on the sides of you all the time, that is what I love about these open roads. And of course, fellow competitors pass me as well but very rarely now as most of them are far ahead or far behind. The race is stretching out now and as time goes by, we are all moving at different speeds, widening the gaps between us. When they do pass me, it seems they do so in an extremely competitive spirit as if the finish line is just up ahead a few miles, and that's okay as well. I am looking forward to passing them in the end, one way or another; maybe.

    I do pass a lot of cars and see vacationers staring out the windows as I come up on them and fly by. Of course, I spend a lot of energy looking in their vehicles before passing them, seeing if they are going to pose any threat to me. Are they focused forward? Are they young or old? Are their kids or phones distracting them? Do their cars seem to be in good running and maintained order like any flat tires? I have seen people drive for miles on flat or very low, dangerous tires. I pass slowly most of the time for all slower moving vehicles as not to scare the drivers, instead weaving and changing lane positions a little so they might notice me in a rear-view mirror. Sometimes they do and stare over at me, which causes them to drift into my lane. Not good but I guess that should be taken as a compliment that they are looking and see me. "Hey, you in the tin can, get your eyes back forward on the road there, nothing to see here! I mean doesn't everyone have beat up old cop bikes without shocks they race down the road?" It has to be wondered what they really think of us 2-wheel types. Sometimes I do wonder if they think I am a cop, maybe dangerous outlaw who doesn't give a crap about safety or others just plowing up the asphalt on this road? Middle aged underemployed rebels with too much time on his hands? Maybe, they are totally envious jealous types who only wish they could let it all go and learn to ride to get away from their everyday life and stress? I have no idea but damn I hope they see me and don't run me over today, or any day, like EVER! No matter how much the American folklore cowboy image races through anyone minds we, and I am still very human and fragile and, break easily. Occasionally I catch them with their camera phones taking pictures of me and my 'differently odd looking' purpose-built race machine. They can be seen with their cameras or phones in their hands pointed at me as they curiously hang out or against windows, with their tongues a lickin'. They all look as if they are watching T.V., kids on their electronics, parents talking or yelling at each other, they just seem to be passing through the scene instead of being part of it.

It has been well written in Robert Pirsig's book: "Zen, and the Art of Motorcycle Maintenance" how many people riding in their cars are simply observing the surroundings and the open road from their car windows, like watching it on a T.V. screen. They are simply trying to get from point A to point B in the quickest time possible without having to be bothered by all of the, in-between. On a motorcycle, I can see it all, I am part of it, totally IN the scene. That road just a few inches beneath my feet is real and the temperature of the great outdoors and all wind is very real as well. If you ever want to know all about my personal reasons for riding and racing, feel free to read the first 3 chapters of Persig's book. If you do not finish reading it that is okay, but you would have to read most of the book to figure out why that is.

I usually get waves and thumbs up from truckers and I always do my best to wave back. Those guys are much bigger and heavier in their rigs than I and, fortunate for me, most of them ride. They usually have and show respect for us little 2 wheeled types flying by them. I always do my best to get along with them, on or off the road. Them and their big arse rigs with the monster trailers bombing down the highways of America, bringing us just about every consumable product imaginable. Oh, sure we move a ton by train and by ship these days, but then it all goes into, or on, a truck and delivered to a store. That's where we, the consumers, purchase it and consume to our little heart's desire. The great American road infrastructure was funded by future money from these monster machines and put together for their use. They just move our economy and our goods from here to there and back again. Without these big boys on the roadway with me, I would not have fuel in my tank, snacks to munch on or a road to ride on. I am simply a small fish in a big ocean of big rigs soaking up the scrapes from their economic industry and I thank them every chance I can for this. The hard working, hard driving, men and women of this country who move us and their tax paying dollars funding this infrastructure of roads I get to run on.

#6

I can see a few other racers in my rear-view mirror catching up to me. I do my best to make out who they are and try to make a game of it to entertain myself. These small games are important as they will assist my mind in staying as sane as possible for the duration of this journey. One is moving faster than the others a mile or two behind me, from my shaking and vibrating mirror a lot of detail is lost. I lean my machine over into the right-hand lane, so they have room to pass. I see now, it's Mrs. Miyagi, a woman in her late 40s maybe, with the kindest heart and warmest smile you could ever know. She reminds me of a preschool teacher I had once upon a time, flying by me at what must be 100 miles per hour on her righteous built Yamaha. She's very concentrated but looks over at me and waves as she humbly passes like a demon on fire with her rain suit flapping in the wind and full-face helmet disguising her true soft nature. She is twisting that fucking throttle and really getting some as she passes my slow arse.

Steve Earle, "The Devil's Right Hand." *Copperhead Road,* Uni Records/ MCA, 1988

At the starting line this morning, she and husband Mr. Miyagi had some trouble with their skoots, as a few other competitors did, while the rest of us left the parking lot. I have no idea what was wrong, but I don't care. They obviously reinstated their badassery to all us other competitors as they fixed it and she is now flying by most of us. He must be moving slower or still at the starting line, again, I just don't really care. She has left her old man in the dust apparently or maybe it's the other way around? I was off the highway for a few minutes, so I just don't know but I am sure she is leading him on this one. What a couple, competing against each other, good for them and I take note appropriately. They are grown arse adults with a lot of time in the saddle, seasoned veterans to this race, they just flat out rock as a power couple. And no, Miyagi is not their real names, just a good nickname he acquired some years back. His true name is Steph Brooks I think, but nobody knows him by that name as some years back I coined the phrase in a discussion amongst fellow Stampeders of "Who the hell is Steph Brooks"? Someone even had some good stickers made, ya can find them on some of our machines.

This is a wonderful road, one of the smoothest in the country I am sure. I have flown over a lot of road in this country, a lot of it on this skoot and wow, what a great four-laner divided beneath me. Maybe it has just been re-paved or maybe, the rhythm of my skoot is keeping with the rhythm of the bumps and imperfections of this road in perfect harmony. Sometimes I get lucky and it's just happens that way, other times not so much. I just have to stop thinking and do nothing but enjoy this moment and all the universe has blessed me with on this perfect road, if even just for a minute as I know this does not, and will not, last for long. The weather is warming nicely, and I just can't complain about anything. There is a big rig in front of me a quarter mile or so and I am gaining on it fast. I go to lean left to will my machine into the passing lane while enjoying this wonderfully smooth road then, BOOM!!!!

Bob Marshall

I watch in slow motion as one of the trailer's rear left tire blows, exploding right in front of me with the thundering sound of a cannon shooting straight and true. I see pounds of steel belted rubber flying into the air in long strip of what used to be the tread of the tire, gators flying everywhere. It's all 100 feet in front of me and yeah, I'm heading straight for it. In a desperate act of instinct, I throw my right foot up and cover the rear brake pedal, like it is going out of style. I start playing out in my head where all this gator looking shrapnel will be flying and landing. I keep my left course hoping I can avoid it all as, the left side shoulder of the left lane looks to be clear. Now I get to start fighting my urge to see the effect of the tread hitting the ground and start doing my best to look towards the safety, not the danger. From my years of experience and a little forced self-training I know that if I simply just look at the safest route and avoid my human instinct to rubber neck at the coolness of destruction, my skoot and my body will follow my eyes. However, if I look at the danger, I will run right into it and it will run right into me, 'dead reckoning' is what they call that, and damn what a fierce bitch it is. I feel my body tense and my breath stop as I start my path in hopes of getting out of this maze of gators without too much damage.

I see past the first piece on my right side, then a second smaller piece I run right over on purpose. It slaps my frame, maybe my exhaust and engine and then slaps my left foot and sends a shock of tingling pain up my leg as I hear and feel that WHACK! I actually purposely hit this piece because now - now I am in a full tire brake aiming my bike towards the truck itself to avoid, THE BIG ONE. The big fat momma of them all that decided to head to the outside of the left lane where I had been praying on for my sanctuary. Like a martyr of disappointment and destruction, it dances straight up in the air as to mock me and my efforts to avoid it. My clutch is held taut in my left hand,

I ease off the rear brake and look a few feet left of the trailer. I am heading straight for its left side. Another piece I could not see almost floating in the air hits my headlight and I feel the bang in my handlebars that I am now death gripping, hoping that THE BIG ONE does not fall my way as it is still dancing in the air, or so my peripheral vision tells me. I feel it pass on my left side. It does not touch me or my machine. I push over to the left now as I look more to the clear road to avoid the side of that big arse trailer.

I release my clutch only to realize yeah, still in high gear and have slowed a lot, even slower than the big rig is moving so my bike kicks back and groans as to say to me: "Hey asshole, I don't have this much compression to accelerate in this gear you fucking idiot!" Pull in the clutch, let off the throttle, downshift twice with a click-click, let the clutch out easy and I start to breathe again and move forward. I look in my rear-view mirror to see gators all over the highway. THAT BIG ONE has fallen to rest and, the riders that were half a mile behind me start swerving and ducking around the debris in a ballet of, 'oh shit let's not die today' maneuvers. I can't imagine what my own little, 'oh shit let's not die today' maneuver must have looked like to them. Pulling alongside the rig, up-shifting as needed, breathing now, I motion to get the driver's attention. He rolls down his window and I yell to him "HEY, you lost a rear tire!"

"WHAT?!?" the driver yells back. I set the throttle lock with my right hand then motion a spinning circle then an explosion with both my hands then, point to the back of his rig with my thumb. He waves and mouths "Thank you" to me as he slows down to stop on the side of the highway. Upshifting now into top gear, I breathe a little easier and get back to moving forward.

"WOW," I yell to myself in my helmet, he did not even feel that explosion or hear it. He must have thought it was just a bump in the road, but to me it was one of the most violent and scary three seconds of my life. Note; If you have never talked or yelled inside a helmet, try it sometime. You will hear yourself louder and clearer than ever before but, with a strange cloudy overtone. It's enough to let yourself scare, well, yourself. I have to wonder if everyone else hears themselves as loud as I do inside that face shield of mine. I mean it's only a face shield, not a full helmet and damn my voice seems loud at any volume. Arlo Guthrie was correct in his singing, "I don't want a pickle, I just want to ride on my motorsickle. And I don't want to die, I just want to ride on my motorcy-cle".

Arlo Guthrie, "The Motorcycle Song." *Alice's Restaurant,* Reprise Records, 1967

I light a smoke and check my old overalls to make sure I did not piss myself or worse. Damn I need to be careful or get lucky out here and not die. This is all very real, and my precious fragile human body will only take so much. I just need to be good to myself in all of this damnit. Nope, I'm good, did not piss or, anything else myself. And no, my overalls are not attractive by any means but, they keep pressure off my bladder for the long 3 or 4 hours I have in seat time between my fuel and coffee stops. I had my Aunt Martha who lives next door sew some cool pleather shin guards on them to deflect weather and motor oil. Yup, I look ridiculous and fatter than I really am but, they work well for this venture and I don't really care how I look. This is after all, blah blah a race, not a fashion show. Luckily, I did not lose any bodily functions back there, but I should have. I relax and let my thoughts drift to other situations and people on my mind as I sip my coffee and enjoy my smoke at a comfy 80 miles per hour. I am sure whatever the speed limit is in this area or any area I am simply hovering a mile or 2 an hour below it. It's posted and, it's the law so I will go just under, 'that fast' if anybody happens to pull me over with flashing lights and asks.

It's funny how naturally I work so hard to control my destiny and when faced with real danger, all I can do is my very best and hope it is good enough. Of course, I really truly have no control over anything, but it makes me feel good to get through this incident as I have gotten through so many before - relying heavily on my natural instinct or maybe even a 6th sense of sorts. I am biased towards this theory of a 6th sense as a family trait, I have seen it in action many times but especially in my Pops. It may sound like a lot of hocus pocus magic, and with no real science to back it up, it's always when for example, that old pan turned knuckle Harley engine almost falls on his head and he moves just right to avoid it and it slams on the top of his tool box. Or when we were driving down the calm residential road and a car comes at us out of control and he commands his station wagon like a race car driver, missing collision by inches. My favorite was when he was delivering an old Harley to me. He pulled up in his Ford, or leather appointed Lincoln, truck with large car trailer that he used for hauling all sorts of machinery for his business. There on the back was a 1984 FLH that was all fully dressed and complete. We unstrapped it and in his lazy sense of getting things done in the most efficient manner, he grabbed a crowbar and started prying the front wheel out of the wheel chalk he had installed on his big arse trailer just for this bike. A quick note: at this time my Pops and I were not racing like we do now and, refused to trailer anything, anywhere. Not a big deal, but we ride everywhere and we're very novice at trailering skoots. So, I was holding the bike up and he perched, or sat up on the toolbox on the front of the trailer, he inserted the crowbar and pulled, then the bar slipped. With the grace of a dancer he slowly fell backwards turning his body slightly and hit the ground with a 'thud' barely missing his head on the tow hitch of the trailer. "Ouch!" is all I heard, long deep and drawn out as I threw down the kickstand on the bike and ran to see him wedged between the arse of his truck and frame of the trailer. Slowly and surely, he worked his way out of space and stood up, not a damn thing wrong with him. From my vantage point I thought for sure he had slammed his body on every frame member and hit is head on the bumper or something. Nope, he missed it all and jumped right up after landing on his back.

My Pops was 62 at the time, 5'10, a little built but carried that belly weight that screams to society: "Yes, I have done VERY well for myself in this life and I LOVE DONUTS"! How he survived and came out of that fall without a scratch is just beyond me, I mean totally beyond my comprehension. I have noticed the same instincts in my younger brother as well as myself. Dangerous things try to hit us or stop us, and we somehow can move and avoid them just right, at just the right moment in time. It's a good skill to have in a bar fight or operating a skoot out here on the open road. I may be wrong but for now, it is simply referred to as; my families 6th sense, the Marshall 6th sense.

This land is climbing now. The road gets a little winding as large plateau topped formations start rising up all around reminding me, I am still in a desert. Even though I have not been here in a few years, the land around me starts to change into a place far away from my known home. I remind myself that this is all America, a part of the world where I am a citizen and pay my taxes. It may seem unfamiliar to me, but many people have been here before. Men and women from a time long ago when exploring was a dangerous game and maybe they survived and maybe, they didn't. They would leave their homes, mothers, wives and children to go out and explore the great west of this land and here I am kicking arse and flying fast by it. Those pioneers had a real spirit and where true bad asses. Today few parts of this this world have not been explored or pioneered by mankind. It is all mapped and given lines and roads, numbers and names. It may still be to me a wild land but, I am sure these days there are many who simply call it their backyard, with a highway running through it.

Oscar Isaac, Marcus Mumford, The Punch Brothers, "Dinks Song, Fare Thee Well." *Another Day, Another Time: Celebrating the Music of Inside Llewyn Davis.* Warner Music Group, 2013.

Yeah, this classic folk song has been around a while, first recorded in 1909 by John Lomax. This version is my favorite, with Chris Thile on mandolin; damn that guy defines playing the mandolin beyond known human comprehension, and I dig every note of it! Did I mention I majored in music in college and the mandolin IS my favorite instrument to play? Yes, I identify as a mandolin player, not the best, but damn I have a lot of fun making that cool instrument sing in my hands.

#7

I can really feel the road now, slowly getting tuned into it all. I can feel the land, the weather, the air flying past me, and my machine is running perfectly with me astride it. Perfectly in tune with all of it, completely part of all of it, my Zen. This may seem a bit intense to state but I have learned over the years that it really does take me several hours of riding to gain complete Zen in what I am actually doing. A short ride to the Colorado River from my home in Southern California has always proven to be a bad idea. As soon as I get there for a bike run or something, I want to keep going as I truly feel I have just gotten the right amount of time to get in touch with the road, my machine and my body, all working together for one common purpose; moving forward as fast and efficiently as possible, or as fast and efficiently as my machine and this road will let me and right now; that's equals a pretty darn good click.

Robert Earl Keen, "The Road Goes on Forever And The Party Never Ends." *West Textures,* Sugar Hill Records, 1989.

I have time to really think now, to process all I want at my leisure. My mind starts to wander. I think about my family, my Pops with my handsome son I left at the starting line. I think about my new girlfriend Ella I left there as well. My mother and little sister even showed up to see me off. I suspect after the race took off that they all went across the parking lot to the diner to let my Pops buy them all breakfast. I can hear him now, "We are the men son, we always pay!" I have to wonder if I am concerned about my family embarrassing me in front of Ella or am I actually wondering how breakfast tasted? I'll do my best to concentrate on the latter as we can never control other people, will have to leave it all up to the universe at this point. I mean, even if I was there enjoying a fat side of bacon with my biscuits and gravy, I would not be in control of all embarrassing comments my family could and would make around me because that's what family is for, right? Control, damn control is always an illusion for us. We never truly have it no matter how hard we try. Control over this machine or the road or the meeting of my new girlfriend with my mom. Yup, totally out of control I am, pretty much all the time, but watch me try to compete.

For this race we all had to check in yesterday, a day before the race, by 4 p.m., get through tech inspection, pony up our money and get our race numbers. Lucky for me I got to retain my lucky number already hand painted on my big arse headlight by Charlie a few years back, # 27. Every competitor is issued a number for his headlight, it's kind of incognito that way. We also got the route and had our racers meeting at 6 p.m. The meeting was basically a few minutes on the hot black asphalt of the parking lot, El Nomad Charlie talking and handing out the route while reinstating the 4 rules of the race. These 4 simple rules that govern us with a few sidebar religious convictions that keep us going, handed down to us from The Gospel according to El Nomad Charlie himself from the pages of a chop mag.

By design the Stampede is a chopper race where our rules are designed to keep it as such, and they are:

1.   Rigid frames only! Struts are okay as long as there is no rubber mount in said strut, this is a chopper race.

2.   No hard bags, no windshields, no bullshit. Again, this is a chopper race.

3.   Every man (or woman) for themselves. No chase vehicles are allowed. This includes other riders who are not competing, especially swing arm bikes.

4.   No rubber mounted engines of any variety are allowed.

We will all follow the same route which will be backed up with fuel receipts. Most everyone that makes it out for the race has the integrity to keep to this plan, but this keeps it honest. This race is illegal, immoral, dangerous, kind of stupid, and a hell of a lot of fun, everyone runs it at their own risk. We are completely unsanctioned, unsponsored and as real as a toothache. People have wrecked, died, blown up engines, destroyed their bikes, been stranded, soaked, lost, and generally been screwed but we all remain undaunted. That being said, to each his own, you ride at your own risk. The road goes on forever and the party never ends.

So, the meeting in the parking lot goes on with El Nomad Charlie stating to us the basics of the race as well as a slew of other good updates on known weather for the route, tips and tricks and the subtle reminder that this race, DOES NOT EXIST! All lean, mean and built 130 pounds of him jumping in our faces about it and appropriately so. We are all in agreement. The sanctity of what we do cannot be understated, to keep ourselves safe from so much confusion in this world of the general public and Johnny Law we have to guard our race as much as humanly possible. This race is not legal, moral or in any way, safe. It's a bad idea and no one should be participating but, there we were, coming from near and far to stand in a hotel parking lot and get the route map and the talking to. F Bomb gave a classic talk as well to all of us on what we all would REALLY think of a competitor who got beat by him on the little 250cc Miss Lorri skoot. He will be moving slower than most, so don't get caught finishing the race behind him. Then a few wagers amongst us competitors were set for the fastest bike below 750cc, the 750cc class, the 1000cc class that I personally got some action on, and the big Harley types as well. I think a few other bets were set also like middle place, how many of us will really finish, and last place, etc. Lots of bills got thrown around and the race was set. In 11 hours, all the uncontrollable madness known as the Stampede Cross Country Chopper Race would begin.

Jimi Hendrix "All Along the Watchtower" by Bob Dylan. *Electric Ladyland,* Reprise, 1968.

So it all started for me and mine a few days ago on Friday when my Excursion of a truck got loaded up with camping gear and hitched up my land speed racing trailer, complete with my land speed racing skoot and 3 bicycles for good measure for some classic family fun on the playas of El Mirage. For us weird enthusiasts of speed and all things that go fast, El Mirage is a dirty mecca, where many a past generation of man and machine have been pushing ever farther in the quest for speed on the dirty old dried up flat lakebed in the Southern California Mojave Desert. Yeah, I like to compete in a few different types of racing. Land Speed racing out at El Mirage is almost as cool as racing at the Bonneville Salt Flats in the northwest part of Utah where we get to really open up the throttles and see just how fast our purpose machines can go. Lately, unfortunately the local potash mine has been taking so much salt off of the Bonneville Salt Flats without replacing or pumping it back that we have not been able to race there. The Bureau of Land Management has done such a piss poor job at regulating the salt flats that in the near future the state of Utah wants to take it over, damn I hope they do, or just give it to us racers to manage. Losing a great treasure like the Bonneville Salt Flats to bureaucracy and corporate greed would be a terrible slap in the face for mankind and our planet, I employ everyone to jump on a skoot or pack up the kids and pets, get a cooler full of sandwiches and head to a time trial event, either at El Mirage or Bonneville, or both. Enjoy the fastest cars and skoots in the world right in front of your eyes, pushing for glory in their quest for speed. Only then will you ever be able to truly understand the magic and speed of these holy grounds; but I digress.

Friday morning, my Pops meets me at my house, mounted himself behind the steering wheel of my rig with my 9-year-old Crew Chief (my son) and my 14-year-old nephew visiting from Oklahoma thrown in for good measure. I threw my girlfriend Ella on the back of this Cross-Country Chop and off we all went to have a Saturday morning run at El Mirage. The playas is a simple several square miles of flat dirt located north of Riverside by the desert town of Adelanto. Lucky for me, it was halfway between Riverside and Barstow, where the Stampede race would start. We just had to leave a day early and do some land speed racing before some cross-country chopper racing right? I am a genius!

For one weekend a month, several months out of the year, the Southern California Timing Association or S.C.T.A. gathers for a meeting of the clubs and to set some land speed records. I am a member in good standings with the S.C.T.A. race club known as the Roadrunners, out of Riverside, California but no, I do not hold a land speed record; yet! I am not the world's fastest anything, but I am getting closer, competing and having a good time with the science and family fun of it all.

So, we got up to the Playas of El Mirage, got the bike all checked in and passed tech inspection. I gave the S.C.T.A. my 100 dollars to race and the camping began. My Pops, my son and my nephew slept in my Excursion while Ella and I slept on an air mattress under my instant pop up. After a good walk to the middle of the long flat racecourse in the dark, hundreds of yards from anyone, yeah, I totally had sex with her out there, and sure, again on the air mattress. I slept like a child that night in the cool desert air, holding that woman's beautiful body. Then it was up and at 'em for a run down the course.

AC/DC "Thunderstruck" *Live at Donington,* Albert, Atco 1990.

Originally, I got into land speed racing as a newly single dad a few years back, as something I could do with my Pops and my son. After a trip we all took in my Excursion up to Bonneville to spectate, it was decided, the Marshalls could and would do this; we can and will land speed race. I know there is a lot of money and speed in this sport, but I saw some good loopholes in all of that with my mechanical ability where for just a few thousand bucks, racing could be had.

Land Speed racing works differently than most might think. First ya get everything ready to race in the pits then, you drive yourself, your skoot on the trailer and your chase vehicle over to the start line and wait in a very choreographed line for your turn on course. After an hour or so of waiting, you are near the front of the line where you put your suit and gear on, start and warm up your bike, get your bike off the trailer. Then ya get to the starting line and wait for Jill Shannon or one of the other fine starters who are running the course to motion to you with a wave of their arms and the course; is yours.

My bike is idling between my legs with both feet on the ground and my chase vehicle behind me and all the waiting has led to this, go time in the world of speed. Oh man how I dream of Jill waving her arms at me, 2 pumps then a motion to close my face shield, then 2 pumps towards the track. The course is all mine for those several seconds on the clock as I jam my land speed skoot into first gear, rev it up and take off. With only 1 and a ⅓ mile to get up to speed I have to make it happen quickly. I twist the throttle beating hard on the skoots engine as I jam the shifter at my left foot down through the gears, clutching and twisting, trying to be as efficient as possible. I can barely hear my skoot even with it's wide open exhaust as the land is open allowing the sound to dissipate and my big leather suit shuts out all wind and feeling of my speed. No, I don't have a speedometer on this bike either, I mean that's what I pay the S.C.T.A. for. The only place I can feel anything land speed racing is between my legs, and I have to concentrate hard to feel what that engine is doing and how to react accordingly.

On this run I was really getting a good start in when all of the sudden, the bike started to burp, and the power started to fumble. I let off the throttle than twisted again as it gave me a little response, I knew something was terribly wrong. I get up to the last gear and played with the throttle some more but could not get the bike out of its fumble as the bike and I limped through the timing gate at like 90 miles per hour. Damn what a disappointment. I knew something had to be wrong with the carbs and or fuel but, I also knew we had no time for another run as I had to get up to Barstow to check in for the Stampede. I would figure out later that somehow one of my floats in one of my carbs got stuck and was allowing the air box to fill up with fuel, causing the bike to run way too rich and basically drown out my poor little land speed racer of a skoot. Well, that's racing, sometimes ya win, sometimes ya compete, and sometimes ya just fall flat on your face shield.

My totally rebuilt land speed racer is a 1980 XJ650 shaft drive Yamaha model I scored as a basket case from a friend for 200 bucks. Thanks Amigo Adam, you are a good one. No paperwork needed as land speed racing is not done on the highway so yearly registration and ownership paperwork is pointless. Possession is 9/10th of the law. I rebuilt the engine to make sure it was all tight, assembled it, tuned it and set it up for S.C.T.A. rules and regulations including a set of high-speed tires that had to be shaved. Now when I say rules and regulations what I mean is, the craziest, most over redundant set of rules a racing organization could ever have. Usually we rebuild and setup skoots for D.O.T. regulations that is, as the Department of Transportation sets the rules for vehicles for highway use; ya know; blinkers, horns, speedometers, yeah like half the crap I am missing on this skoot now but for going as fast as possible in a straight line, that skoot has to be setup on a very different set of rules while passing a rigorous inspection before every meet. It's all in the name of safety at high speed, my Pops, my little dude and I, okay mostly me, had a great time figuring out all the rules and building a bike in just a few months that passed inspection the first time out. So, I put down 200 smackers for the bike, maybe another 200 in engine gaskets, carb jets and safety items like a steering damper and hand grips. Hand grips can be so overrated sometimes, if you aren't crossing the country on the skoot, some hockey stick tape works just fine but, real handgrips it is for the land speed racer skoot as it's all part of the rules. Also, there was 700 bucks in the tires, I had to buy them then, have them installed on the rims and shaved down so the tread would not come flying off at high speeds. Luckily there is a one stop shop for this over in Signal Hill California called 'Cowboy Tires' and Nate there does some good work.

My Pops rebuilt our old jet ski trailer by lowering the axle and setting a large 8 inch heavy duty U channel piece of steel right down the middle, with the assistance of a ramp, that's where we roll the skoot up to and it sits on the U channel. He even painted it and when I say he, I mean he owns a small machine building business so he had his guys do it, but I am sure he watched and told them how to do it right as the engineer he is. Then I added some new tires and an old chrome truck bed toolbox to the front of it complete with bicycle rack so, yay, just a few hundred bucks in that as well.

Then came my racing suit. It had to be all leather with no perforations (a rule I think they did away with these days) so usually people had them custom made for several thousand dollars. I purchased one from an online store for a few hundred then handed it to my younger brother who does leather work on the side. He expanded the chest of the suit for my large bulk by adding leather under the armpits then added leather to the crotch, for my large set of balls or, so I could straddle the seat on the skoot comfortable. The best part was he had a lot of perforations to cover up, which most people do with strips of leather. My brother, in all his creativity, added metal studs to cover all these holes. So yeah, I look like Elvis in my suit but it passes regulations and after the initial cost and a side of cow plus metal studs, a full face approved helmet on sale for 200 bucks, some fully covering leather gloves and a set of Doc Marten boots, I was only out a thousand bucks or so for all that.

Hitching it all up to the Excursion that has been around for many years and my flying circus of a motley race team is complete. Yes, it does cost to keep it all going. I have managed to subsidize racing by selling the parts I take off my skoots via eBay. It's only a few grand a year and I have a few more hundred in small sponsorships but, it's good family memories and comparable to what most people pay these days to enjoy more corporate or popular things with their children and family. Mine is just dirty, on the cheap and all about going fast in a straight line for a few minutes then, camping in the dirt. Land speed racing has got to be the most unpopular sport in the world, and I have no idea why.

Did I mention how big the Bonneville salt flat is? It is so big, flat and white that astronauts used it as a marker on earth when they are up flying around in space and doing what those cool people do. My personal interest in the sport started many years earlier as a young man when my Pops, in his many travels as a salesman, had gone to the speed mecca of the world to check out an S.C.T.A. event. He brought me back a postcard of a racer standing in front of his race car which looked nothing like a car to me and these crazy high numbers of speed records were printed on this card. I remember thinking to myself how the heck could anyone get such a funny looking vehicle to go that fast. And as they say, 'nothing was ever the same again.'

Fast forward many years to my early thirties when my Pops and I loaded up on our cool Honda cruisers with some clothing and snacks and set off for the Bonneville speed week event. The journey was only 600 miles or so but it took us 2 days to get there fighting heat, overloaded bikes and my Pops having to stop in Las Vegas to collect a business check for half a million dollars or some crap like that, it totally got in our way of being awesome road warriors on our mission to spectate speed. My dad, always letting business be important, damn I wish I had a dollar for every time he was on the side of the road on his skoot, with the phone to his ear, on a damn business call.

Pops rode his newer 2004 Honda 1300 V.T.R. a cool black model he had purchased a few months earlier. I got to go and pick it up for him because of course he was out of town on business when he bought it sight unseen and it was up to me to determine if it was worth purchasing. What a foolish notion for him to trust the likes of me, with such responsibility. It really was a wonderful machine complete with windshield and sissy bar for all the crap he wanted to bring and ready for the open road, as well as any or all apocalyptic events and maybe a complete breakdown of civilization or an alien encounter. Damn my Pops can pile that thing high.

I was no better in the packing of my 2000 Honda VT1100 Shadow, also complete with windshield and sissy bar, with bags, camping gear, cooler, and 2 Stanley coffee urns for good measure. Wow, what the heck were we thinking? I can tell you these days I travel A LOT lighter. Even if I had to camp, a gas station or food joint is never far away, don't need as many clothes because what's the point? I don't mind stinking a little out here in the wind and there are no ladies to impress or, none I want to impress anyways -- usually. I am a dedicated man these days to one Miss Ella. Besides, there are laundromats or even general stores everywhere, if I need to buy more clothes. For this race, I am probably one of the most loaded down on my skoot but, I am confident I am carrying only what I need. For starters, I carry a general clothing bag, it's about 16 inches wide and 12 inches tall, dark brown, pleather, old and worn. It rides between my headlight and handlebars under my jacket unless I happen to be wearing my jacket. The bag contains:

A set of blue jeans and my belt as I am currently wearing my overalls, planning on enjoying some good ole blue jeans at the finish line.

2 long sleeve t-shirts, my preferred riding under garb to keep the sun and weather off of my arms.

- 1 short sleeve cotton t shirt; ya know I just seem to be able to buy a good short sleeve shirt anywhere so why carry them.

3 spare boxer briefs.

3 sets of lighter socks. I prefer the heavy socks when I ride and am wearing them now. They were a gift from my mistress that keeps out more weather and seems to add a little shock absorption in these old worn boots of mine.

Chuck Taylor type tennis shoes and my cheap sandals.

A spare, small towel for a quick pits and crotch shower.

My Dopp kit. Yes, full to the brim with all extras I might need and then some. I keep it right on top by the zipper so I can access anything out of it as needed.

Bob Marshall

My Dopp kit holds:

- Small toothbrush and small toothpaste
- Bag balm for dry skin
- Extra sunscreen
- Small deodorant
- Eye drops
- Painkillers
- Vitamins
- Earplugs; for sleeping next to the highway
- Q tips; like a 30 pack, very important for cleaning out my ears, nose, and most motorcycle parts.
- Band aids and mouthwash; for some first aid as needed.

Then I have my small tank bag. It works well and I fiddle with it often to reorganize it and keep it working for me.

In it I have:

- Dark or tinted Goggles
- Clear goggles
- Yellow goggles
- Clear glasses
- Dark glasses

- Lip balm; s.p.f. 15 with a touch of mint so I can shove some up my nose if needed and aid in breathing issues should any such issues occur.

- My super heavy leather gauntlet gloves

- 1 extra set of light leather workman's gloves

- Spare lighters

- Mini Mag Flashlight

- Spare batteries AAA for my flashlight and mp3 player

- Spare ear buds

- Sunscreen; mini tube

- Snacks like trail mix or beef jerky and small hard coffee candies

- Blue nitrile gloves for really cold riding

- Dry towel to wipe rain from my eyes while riding

Yup, it's a lot to fit in a small tank bag but everything has its place and it works well for me. As I go down the road, I can reorganize it as needed or as a distraction to assist in keeping my mind awake. Sometimes keeping the stuff from falling out or blowing away is half the battle. Next I have a smaller set of saddlebags under my seat for tools and spare parts. I can rip the bike apart with all the tools and carry a spare of everything important like a coil, clutch cable, throttle cable, nuts and bolts, etc. Then I have my big black bag in the passenger's seat behind me. What's in the big black bag you might ask? I mean I am already really carrying everything I could ever need and then some right? The answer is, THE SUIT! The suit is a large, insulated full covering for all weather riding. It takes up the space of a 0-degree sleeping bag and doubles as a sleeping bag when needed. Most of the other racers carry some or all the needed rain gear and warmer gear like leather jackets or maybe chaps. I have tried leather but I got-to-tell ya, after an hour or two of really hauling arse and riding in it, it just becomes cold in the cold or hot in the heat. Yes, it's true; leather can and will save your arse if you find yourself sliding on the pavement but it's heavy and cumbersome, so for this trip, I opted to leave most of it at home. If I need to be warm, I carry it all in one big black and green suit, with some reflective materials for good measure. I also had my aunt sew some pleather guards on the front of the legs, so I look like a big black puffy marshmallow man when I wear; the suit. I don't mind this because it will able me to travel through very cold temperatures and very wet conditions or both. All I have to do is pull over on the side of the road, give myself 5 minutes to zip it on and adorn my vest over it and bam!

Oh, those bags in the cages...so when the cop bikes were originally built by Kawasaki, it was important that they could do almost anything, and go almost anywhere, and be bulletproof about it. Yes, they even came with bullet proof tires that did not deflate when punctured. So, of course having some cool cages around the original saddle bags was very important. $7/8$ chrome bars that I wrapped in bungee netting because a big rule of this race is, we cannot have hard bags. I have a small soft bag on the left side holding my chain lube and wax, some air filter oil, a hammer, some tire spoons and above all, my oil. Yup, I'm losing a little oil, just under a quart every 1000 miles currently. I can see in the lower part of the left casing where it is leaking from but did not fix it before this race. I'm just carrying a few quarts and a funnel to add as needed. I use a very well-known racing oil that is not cheap but, as with most things, I feel good and view it as cheap insurance to invest a few extra dollars for the good stuff.

Sometimes I even get it for free or at a very discounted rate, one of the only perks being in the world of motorcycle racing and having good friends like Steve Adams who doesn't mind throwing a little sponsorship my way. Sure, sometimes I miscalculated the amount of oil I will go through on a trip and end up picking up another motorcycle oil or even some diesel truck oil. As long as it is all synthetic and has no molly or graphite in it, it can be used, no regular car oil allowed in skoots.

For this race I was able to secure a few good sponsors. Sponsorship always seems to work differently for people. F Bomb is not the biggest fan of having sponsors, it gives him commitment to people he does not want to owe anything too at the end of the day that makes a lot of sense. So, if ya see a name on him or his skoot for any reason, it's because he likes you or maybe you are a friend that has hooked him up with some goods. Then there are others who maybe make a living off of sponsorship and wear the funny shirts and jackets where every square inch is covered with a brand name, good for them! So yeah, none of those types of people are in this race. Don't ask me why, I mean this is the coolest race ever but people who make a living racing are not here. Oh well, to each their own. Then there is me, for the fun of it I always put out that, I am happy to take a little sponsorship if anyone is interested in putting their name or brand on my skoot. I usually wait till the last few weeks before a race to put it out there on my social media or at different skoot based meetings I attend. "Hey everyone, who wants to see their brand name race across the country on a home rebuilt old cop bike that may or may not make it to the other side?!? Give me a small brand sticker and 100 bucks and you are in the club! For 400 bucks I will give you the big main gas tank and paint your logo or brand on both sides."

So far this has netted me several sponsors whose small stickers are on my fenders, engine, and spare fuel cell, even my mom gets in on the action and my girlfriend Ella drew a mom tattoo looking logo on the top middle of my front fender, ya know the heart with the arrow through it that says mom? I was impressed. My main gas tank is still stock and bare, no one had forked over the cash to buy my fuel for the tank for the race and that was okay with me as I do this for fun, not for a living because I got a J.O.B. to assist me in that money stuff.

The more sponsorship you have, the more people expect out of you. I personally view all this as a little kick in the pants to make sure I make it to the starting line, and I had just enough sponsorship to make me get there. I can't lie either as the new girlfriend was terribly impressed with what I did and how I did it. Yeah, getting the starting line this morning was really like half the battle and that battle was won victoriously.

#8

I met Ella several months ago through a group of meetings that she and I attend. These meetings are the type that assist one with their loss and attitude towards not being able to change or control situations. Similar to myself, she was having issues with family and friends and one day she called me to talk something out. I was at work painting an office or something and I just let her talk away. Then she invited me for coffee a few days later, I choose my favorite coffee house in beautiful downtown Riverside called Back to The Grind. Standing out front on University Avenue while leaning against a light pole and thinking to myself, "What is this beautiful young lady doing meeting you of all people Bob?" I am sure she just needs to talk, and we can share and learn from each other. I mean I was technically a single man as my wife had been gone over a year now but that's no reason for her to ask you out to coffee, is it?

Bon Jovi, "Wanted Dead or Alive." *Slippery When Wet,* Mercury Records, 1986

She was of course fashionably late and dressed casually, wearing something that looked like a summertime onesie. She wore it well with a light sweater and 2-inch black heels. She was tall, medium build with a large set of breasts that hit you before her smile did if you weren't careful with your eyes. 5'6 maybe without the heels but 5'8 with them and her long straight flowing black hair complimented her very well. Myself being 6'2, I had always enjoyed a tall woman making herself taller in my presence, but I also learned not to judge a woman by her height or any of her physical attributes if you know what I mean. We got coffee and chai tea and sat inside the coffee shop at a large round, and not to intimate, table placed towards the front door (my choice) and we're there for hours. She cried a lot, we laughed a little, talked, shared and all in all it was a wonderful delightful experience.

When I walked her to her car she asked if she could see me again? 'See me again' I thought to myself, was this 2 people SEEING each other? I agreed she could call me sometime and we will see what works out. I walked back to my skoot in front of the coffee house mumbling to myself, "What the fuck Bob? This young woman has got to be 15 years younger than you." 12 years I figured out later. She was 26 and I was 38, why would she want to see me again? A day or two later she called me, and we were out for coffee at another downtown coffee house. Sitting in front of a large glass windows watching the traffic creep by, laughing and talking, talking and laughing, as two people on a "date" do. I told her of my 2 beautiful children, my funny little house and of course my skoot racing. She told me of her time in college, her new job as a Family Therapist, and the bad issues she had with her own family. As her questions led on and her curiosity piqued about my funny little house, I agreed to just take her there and show her.

Back at my place, I showed her around my property telling more of what I do in my land speed racing and cross country chopper racing, showing her my beat up, well used and loved skoots and the funny little carriage shed I use for a 'Laboratory' to wrench in. Then she attacked me and, well, I did not resist and I kind of attacked her back. Here was this young, beautiful and apparently seemingly intelligent woman attacking me. Yay for me, right? As we fumbled our way to the bedroom and slowly removed our clothing, I could tell something was a little off. I mean the first-time having sex with a new woman will always be a little funny and weird or uncomfortable but this, seemed really uncomfortable. Eventually she told me that she had very little experience with this. "Well that's okay," I proclaimed "let's take our time with it, be good to ourselves about it."

"I mean'" she stated hesitantly, "I have not had actual sex before, with a man."

So, there I was with this beautiful naked woman in my bed and I could not believe what I was hearing. How is it, a 26-year-old outgoing and beautiful woman like this proclaims to be a virgin? I instantly felt like that dirty old man, what was I even doing here? A person will always have crossroads in their life where they must stop and ask themselves if they should go left, right or straight or back on a road. These decisions are always what seems to make or break a person. Setting boundaries and stating moral principles of who they are and how the world will remember them. For me, this was definitely one of those crossroads, and a big arse crossroad at that!

I stopped, just lying there in my bed, holding her while we chatted, and I reminded her it was okay and we would find our road in this. She cried a little and was very thankful for my patience and understanding in this. We got dressed and went out on my porch to enjoy the evening air before she had to get back home to her parents' house, yeah, she was still living with her parents in the next town over the mountain a few miles to the north. I can see Mount Rubidoux from my front porch, the city or township is just on the other side. Before she left, she spoke of all the times with her few previous boyfriends tried to seal this deal with her, but she was just not ready or, something else threw a wrench in it all. Then she spoke of her attraction to women and the female body and I completely agreed with her, I'm a BIG fan of the female body myself. She was telling me that she viewed herself as bisexual. She wanted me, and this not being my first rodeo, I had to do the math and figure out that I had been with six virgins in total in my younger life. I had to be confident in the simple statement that I could be her man -- making her comfortable in relationships and sexuality. Decision made, word spoken; my word to which I will strive to be impeccable with, as usual. A few days and dates out for dinner and coffee later we were at it again, and with some success.

"Am I going to hell for this?" I would have to ask myself several times before we got to this moment. "I mean she is a grown arse woman and I don't need to be the one handling her. She knows what she is doing and right now she wants to do you, Bob!" I was confident I had given her plenty of opportunity to leave me alone, reminding her she owed me nothing but damn it seemed she really wanted me so there I was, 38 exploding the hymen of a 26-year-old woman as she thanked me profusely.

We spent a lot of time together right off in our courtship. Almost every night she was at my house where we were cooking dinner or going out to dinner and coffee then back to my house, etc... She had her standard issues like any 20-something year old would have still living with their parents. She would tell me stories of her and her parents fighting about this that or the other and it all seemed a little rough around the edges for a family, but who am I to judge? I even introduced her to my 8-year-old son, and we did a few weekend activities together. As a children's therapist, she was very good with him and good to him, that is the most any single man and parent like me could of asked for. She made me very happy and was very attentive to me in all appropriate manners.

As I left her back at the starting line with my father and son I was starting to wonder if she got home okay. I am sure she will text me soon to let me know, but if she doesn't, I would have to be okay with that. As communication is the greatest form of compliment I could know, I have learned that sometimes I truly hold it in too much damn regard. It's a reservation I put on myself, as my Pops taught me appropriately to do so, to respond to people and their communications to be as responsible as I can be in this life. Responsibility is the action of responding; by phone, email, carrier pigeon, face to face, whatever. I do my very best, and when others around me do not do the same, I have been known to take it personally and we all know, we should never take anything too personally especially, the actions of others. Just because a person does not respond to me in a timely manner does not mean the end of the day for me. Yes, it has been a problem for me in the past, part of my inventory if you will, and I am well aware of it, always working on it. People will always let you down if you let them but darn if they could get back to me in 24 hours, that would be awesome and appropriate to separate us humans from the apes.

My phone being mounted in a waterproof case on the handlebars, I can see texts and stuff. It all just takes me several minutes sometimes with all the riding and navigating I got going on here as the skoot is vibrating violently and my phone is of course freaking out about it, obviously not too happy. One second of time for the phone, 3 seconds of time for the road, it's a vicious cycle that keeps me entertained. Just a side note; one should never operate a phone while simultaneously operating a moving vehicle. For me it's no different than changing the radio station in a car but for most of us, well we just cannot and should not do it. I grew up with a businessman for a Dad, so I learned to talk on the phone while driving back when his car phone was mounted in his company car, a late 1980s 2 tone Caprice Classic. My phone is mounted on the left of the handlebar, I am left handed, this is the only way I am able to do all I do while riding as I do but please know, most of what I do in this race is not as safe as it could be, this includes operating my phone while racing this chopper cross country.

Some social media posts come in, I will have to wait for another road or just take a minute when I stop to weed through it all and make sense of it. Above all, I know if I post every few hours it will keep my family and friends from worrying about me and that is worth its weight in gold to them and to me. I'm still hoping to hear from Ella soon.

I had purchased Ella an airplane ticket to the other side of the country a few days earlier so she could meet me several days from now when or if I finish this race. Regardless she is flying into Raleigh, North Carolina where my friend Heather, (F Bomb's girlfriend), was renting a car and was happy to give her a ride to where the race was ending. I know all that is weighing heavy on her mind, she was very excited to travel to meet me, but was not sure if she could secure a ride to the airport to get on the flight. She'll figure it all out, I am sure. If I finish this race, she will be there with open arms to greet me. What pure awesomeness that will be to have a partner who shows up, supports and enjoys the after party.

Dire Straits, "Romeo and Juliet" *Making Movies,* Vertigo Records, 1980.

This road is still a few inches beneath my feet, and I can see it is starting to change. I've been on this road before and am aware of what it should look like or maybe, what my mind remembers it looking like. All roads have a rhythm to them as well as a timbre that can be quite unique. I always get the pleasure of paying very close attention to road surfaces, how much rock, asphalt or concrete it was made from, how is the maintenance looking on it, etc. On a rigid frame skoot these small details of the road are extremely important not just for comfort but for handling. A few too many potholes or bad cuts in the road, especially on a banked turn could easily send me undulating off into the weeds if I don't catch it and correct it in a timely manner. The rear of the bike will get into a hop, skip and wobble that can be hard to pull out of. When I find myself in one of these situations, I simply just have to correct or change the angle of the bike and my speed a little, that gets me out of it, well; it has so far anyways. It's just one of those tricks you have to have up your sleeve running on a chopped skoot. All this attention to detail really assists me in keeping my mind sharp and awake. That hard road beneath me will hurt if I hit it, best not to find out how much hurt.

The humidity is rising, the sky is getting grey and I think it is going to rain soon, but I can't see the heavy dark nimbus clouds that usually hover overhead in this situation. But I can definitely feel it and smell it. We'll just have to wait and see what happens. As the humidity rises, the air gets thicker and the skoot starts to push more to get through. I mean, ya fly over a mountain range or something and all of a sudden, it feels like you are swimming in the ocean, not riding in the wind. This is one of my weak points as I live in the well-tempered dry air of Southern California. Pushing through this humid or heavy air is always a challenge for me and my machine. Well, if it all works out, I hope to see or smell a storm before it hits me. I would prefer to put the suit on in the dry weather before the wet weather, but it may not work out that way, "Only time will tell Pinky, only time will tell."

Looking over to my left, Mrs. Miyagi is passing me, again. Good for her. With the concentration of a warrior I can see in her face she is happy to be moving and fast as she passes and waves a little. Most people are passing me, honestly. At my steady pace, most will pass in an attempt to stay at the front of the racers or maybe buy themselves some time for sleep in the future. The animal instinct really comes out of all us racers types at a time like this as we all want to do good and be near the front. As they pass me, I can see and feel the satisfaction they have, and it makes them feel just that much faster or better. Yes, this is a race, and although I am not interested in being last, I am shooting for a more even and steady pace to get me to the finish line, with myself and my machine in one piece.

Occasionally I see a bike or two on the side of the road and most of the time, they are fellow racers who are re-stowing and tightening their gear or maybe they have just broken down and are violently fixing something with knees on the ground, tool pouches open and their hands inside the inner workings of their skoots. I know most of them, but also know they are not on fire, so I won't be pulling over to piss on them. They'll be okay. They are fellow racers and are extremely resourceful. They can fix or rebuild almost anything on their machine, even on the side of the road. Once or twice I pass someone who I don't recognize, just standing there on the side of the road staring at their machines. Competitors who entered this race who may not have the full understanding of their machines. Maybe, they bought them or just have not worked on them much? I can feel their anxiety radiating from them, even at my speed because we have all been there. As the few I saw equally perplexed with their machines at the beginning of the race, they might have to rely on someone else or something else to assist them. I see another competitor there, pulled over to the right side of the road and slam on the brakes.

Mrs. Miyagi is on the side of the road, fiddling with her skoot. I pull over, over-shooting her by 100 feet or so. Knowing this is against the rules I have to make that quick decision and decide to be chivalrous or not. I mean this is my friend, and my friend's wife. I turn off my skoot and walk back to her, helmet and gloves still on. She sees me and as we meet, she tells me a bolt fell out of her frame for her pedal board, but she used some safety wire to re-secure it. I give her a nod in approval. She thanked me profusely for stopping for her and them reminds me this is a race and I need to go. I walk back to my skoot, start it up and take off merging into traffic.

Back on the road now, enjoying the views and cool weather. Ten minutes later, she passes me again, smiles and waves. Oh, how strange this concept of; leaving each other on the side of the road the way we do. It seems we, as Americans are naturally interested in making sure our friends are okay and that we can see them, this is probably why car caravans are so popular as group rides are in motorcycling. For us cross country chopper racers we all know the best thing we can do is leave each other alone unless it's your friends' wife of course. Between all of us, it would not be uncommon to fly by the person you just spent Christmas with. Not on fire, not waving me down = not stopping. For most, we like to have that control, even over our friends but at the end of the day, we have no real control over anything.

Ryan Bingham, "Southside Of Heaven," *Mescalito,* Lost Highway, 2007.

This land is wonderful. Zion National Forest is off to my right, and the scenery is just above anything man could ever conceive or manufacture. God's painting on this beautiful landscape and I am in the thick of it, with no cage or windows around me to obstruct my view, wow, just wow!

Beaver, Utah is in front; the junction to interstate 70 is only 25 miles or so north of that, a town called Cove Fort, I think. That's my road. I need to make that right turn and not miss it. Beaver is a bigger town and may have bigger fuel stops off to the right, easy in and out, faster for me but if I push it 25 more miles to somewhere around the junction it could all equal up to less stops if there is a station near the junction. I slow a few miles an hour and go through Beaver and there it is, a big shiny truck stop off to the right. Crap, I'll take it, I am out of coffee anyways.

I pull off and find my fellow competitor Caleb again at this stop and now he is chatting it up with another fellow competitor. I nod and wave as they hold a casual conversation on an issue Caleb seems to be having with his skoot. Good for them I think, I mean really, they know what this race means to them and they are exercising it well. They want to go fast on the road and enjoy the speed of their skoots. Unless they wear their skoots out from the speed wear and tear then, awesome for me as I might end up finishing before them; only time will tell.

I slide my card, unhook and move my tank bags, and begin my fueling dance with my skoot as my dance partner. Done fueling, I grab the bike and throw it upright to check my oil site glass on the side of the engine. It's a little low, so I pull out the funnel and the rag and oil from my right-side rear bag. I remove the oil fill cap from the top of the engine. Mind you, it's hot as hell and does not always cooperate. The rag is used as insulation, as is my riding glove. Setting up the funnel and opening the oil bottle, slowly pour in a few ounces of the magical lubricating, life giving, mythical blood to the engine. Okay there is no magic to any of it, it's simply science. After finishing, the cap screws back on, and tightly. I replace these items in the tote strategically then grabbing my chain lube from the same tote, I spray the rear sprocket and chain a little. This will be done, or tried to be remembered to be done, every time I stop from now on alternating between chain lube and chain wax as I see fit and the weather allows. If it rains, lube, if the weather is clear, wax. The answer should be -- mostly wax. I am starting with lube because I am sure I forgot to lube the chain at the beginning of this race like I wanted too, shame on me.

Now for some exercise, damn my legs will wear out quickly just sitting like they tend to do while riding. All our bodies are different, but I know stretching and working my legs will keep me going longer as needed, like all that crap my Pops told me would happen in older age is coming true. Damn I really hate that guy sometimes, or just hate it when he is right, as usual! I pick up the bike, kick the kickstand up and push the bike 50 feet or so to a parking stall in front of the convenience store. I am sure this looks ridiculous to other motorists at the station, they all seem to be watching me as I am watching them to make sure they don't run me over. This one action; this minute of pushing my bike will do wonders for me in keeping my body moving well. Alternating which side the skoot is pushed from is a big help but mostly, like most of us, I push from the left side, where the kickstand is and can be kicked up as needed.

Kickstand down, I think for a quick minute and leave the chain lube spray on the seat, grab my coffee tumbler and snug it into my back, right pocket. Walking inside I hit the head and pee then hit the coffee counter to refill. I stop and grab some more water as I will always be nursing that wetness as I ride. I like the

750ml bottles with the sports top that I can pop with my teeth and they are usually on sale if you buy two. Oh, bananas are on sale, and some beef jerky for lunch, pay the clerk at the counter and I am back outside. I stow one water bottle in front of me in the netting I use to hold my bag to my bars. This black netting sure does come in handy for holding everything down, and then some. Sure, it looks a little ridiculous and you can and will hang yourself on it if you aren't paying attention but damn it gets the job done for sure. I bend over and stow the other water bottle in my red snack bag. Oh yes, my snack bag. When I set out on this race, my girlfriend Ella was certain I would need a snack bag. It's understood that I don't stop to eat, just snack; causing F Bomb to refer to my racing outfit as: Team Snackman Racing. I take it as a compliment from the likes of him. I had an extra metal cage on the right side of the skoot so, an old red backpack was re-appropriated, and she half filled it with my trail mix, and then some small candies and her face shield for her helmet. She was okay flying with her helmet but did not want to bother with her face shield and I don't mind having an extra, I guess. Actually, I could really use it right about now after beating mine up at the start of the race, but I'll just keep using mine. The scratches are making for some interesting scenery. Or are they; making the scenery interesting? As I look down in the snack bag I notice, it's already open, damn. Seems I have already lost a few snacks and an extra soft bag I had for a helmet; I think. Honestly, I don't remember if I brought it or not. but whatever, it's race time, got to get my giddy on. I adorn my helmet and gloves, grab the lube, start the bike and take off to the parking lot where I do a few big lazy circles aiming and spraying the lube on the chain as the bike cruises along at a good 1.3 miles an hour. I have this great little space between the chain guard and the engine where the lube hits the hot chain well. Stop, stow the lube back in its tote and off I go, down the ramp and north again. That might of been a 10 minute stop, my competitors are still back at the gas station figuring something out on one of their skoots, we all give each other a wave then its "GO BOB, GO!"

Lady Gaga, "Poker Face." *The Fame*. Streamline, Kon Live, 2008.

Some music my teenage daughter put on my mp3 player a few years back. Last time I ran this race, she had come to the starting line with my wife and son but this year, she was busy in college and I think the whole "Dad taking off for another ride across the country," is old news to her at this point. I got to speak with her on the phone a few days ago and she wished me well. My daughter is a product from my high school days. Her mother was 2 years younger than me. Back then I was a long haired, cross country running, guitar playing, old convertible Cadillac driving well-built dude. We dated for almost a year when she became pregnant. Don't ask me how, but there she was 15 and pregnant and I was sure somehow it was my fault.

Naturally we continued our relationship with the highest hopes of forever and all the good things of that American dream. I even moved in with her at her mom's house and we all lived well as it was a big house. Our daughter was born, she was the most beautiful and precious thing I could of ever imagined. There she was this beautiful perfect child, free of sin but full of responsibility that I knew, would all be worth it. It was the best day of my life so far, I was a dad and damn it I was going to be a good one, my daughter deserved it.

Within a year or so, the relationship I had with my daughter's mom fell apart and there was nothing to do about it. I moved out and into my rock band's house. I slept in the gear storage closet and did my best to continue being dad, my daughter being the center of my world. I worked night and day and went to school. She was the one, that one thing; that one human being who really taught me what love was, what it meant to put someone far above yourself and love without reservation or condition. Yeah, I am a big fan of my 'not so little anymore' daughter.

Several months before this race she had moved back home for a while, to save some money on rent in the college dorms. I was so excited to have her home and she gave me a long speech of what she wanted to pay me and what chores she would take care of, etc. It was just nice to have her home and know she was safe and comfortable. When I started dating my girlfriend Ella shortly after, my daughter was beside herself with me dating a woman only 5 years older than herself. An argument ensued, typical family drama between a smarter than average daughter and her dad. She moved out the next day refusing to stay. I had to let her be mad at me, I had to let her go and find her own way, there was nothing I could say or do about it. Compared to that situation, this chopper racing is a walk in the park on a spring day.

This road race is going well for me, my love life is going well for me, my children are healthy and happy and my skoot is just suck, boom, bang, blowing right along righteously, All I have to do is get there and survive.

#9

Wow, really climbing and winding now, up and up I go, to the left and right, exerting all my effort to stay on the road and in my lane. Sometimes you just hit that point where you are not sure if there is even any road in front of you. One has to trust the highway does not abruptly end. This is like being in a video game only, without extra lives. Last time I was on this road was in the middle of the night and it was a little scarier then. Ready to make the eastward right turn on to interstate 70 here in Utah and into Colorado and the great Rockies. There it is, I take it to the right. I know I will be on this road for a while, across most of this country. It's always amazing how a road with the same number on it can change so much in topography and scenery right in front of me or, underneath me. I'm high on a mountain range now, feeling on top of the world, then: rain. Like small B.B.'s being shot at me, the rain is on my neck where it is felt most and visibility against my face shield. I tightened up the bandana around my neck but it's time to change my plan of attack a little.

Sam Bush, "Whaysay" *Glamour and Grits,* Sugar Hill Records, 1996.

I have to think for a minute on how heavy this rain might be. Will it last a while or will it clear out quickly? The temperature is good, so no chance of freezing if I get a little wet. I see an observing lookout point on my right, the perfect quick pull over place. I pull into it, or on top of it, as it sits several feet above the road. For miles the grey, misty valley below can be seen stretching out to the east. I am being pelted now by big, painful rain drops. I stop, shift into neutral and leave the machine running while I jump off. I undo the black bag on my rear seat and slide my suit out of it. Yes, my chop has its own independently suspended and mounted passengers seat complete with a 12-inch sissy bar. I built it all a few months ago knowing that there might be a passenger on the ride back from this race, so it is mounted and along for the race. An extra 20 pounds with its own seat springs but right now it's just holding onto my suit with the aid of some bungee netting.

Unbuttoning my vest and laying it on my seat with my earbuds dangling from it, I start putting the suit on one leg at a time. There is another competitor Robert; he is pulling over with me but he's over on the shoulder of the road, not up here on the lookout. He smiles and waves as I wave back as we are both dancing with our rain gear. We both have that bothered look in our faces and our body language that says 'crap, now we get to ride through the rain and get wet.' Within minutes I am rebuttoning my vest over my suit, plugging in my ear buds, helmet strapped on, gloved and re-saddled on my skoot. I wave to my competitor, up shifting while twisting some throttle down the on ramp and back onto interstate 70, my new best friend.

Charlie Daniels Band, "The Devil Went Down to Georgia." *Million Mile Reflection,* Epic Records, 1979.

Elevation still going up as this road slowly climbs and my skoot is responding nicely, even in this rain. I had made a bet at the beginning of this race that even though we did not have the route, I was certain it would be in most of this country's higher elevations, so I set the carburetors up appropriately. My cop bike originally came with a 127.5 main jet and stock needles in the carbs. This number and configuration made a lot of sense as it was from San Francisco and at sea level where the fatter or bigger main jets are needed as the air pressure is higher like, 1 whole atmosphere. So, to get the stoichiometry correct at around 14.7 parts air to 1-part fuel, the 127.5 jets worked nicely down there. I have punched this engine out a bit with larger race pistons so it's not really a 1000 cubic centimeter or, 998cc as they really are, I think it's more around 1045, just a millimeter larger per cylinder. I decided to go with a short, older needle off of the old 1100cc engine that Kawasaki used to make and a 100 main jet. The fatter yet shorter needle enables me to get to top speed at half throttle, so I am not killing my wrist or hand. I give it a little twist and it gives me a shit ton of acceleration. This is good for long distance but a hassle in parking lots, where I have to really exercise the clutch to keep it from getting away from me, resting my right-hand thumb on the throttle housing to keep the rear tire from breaking loose on me. It's going to save my wrist in the long run on this race, even though I have a throttle rocker device and a cruise control of sorts. With my main jet being smaller, the engine will have more horsepower in the higher altitudes as the air gets just a little thinner and I may even get a little better gas mileage, in theory anyways. But you can imagine I really don't care about my fuel consumption.

Turnpike Troubadours, "Every Girl" *Diamonds and Gasoline,* Bossier Records, 2010.

The problem with all of this is as I get to the finish line in the lower and more humid and hot south, the heat builds up and it will be harder to keep the engine from running lean; that is, too much air and not enough fuel. That is how an engine runs hot and blows up. I did, however, remember to bring spare jets that are fatter, and if I feel the need, I can change the main jets when I get to that point in the south east side of this country.

In the rain now, I light a smoke and take a swig of coffee getting ready for the worst of it. Riding a rigid chopped skoot in the rain may sound tricky or just out right miserable, but over the years I have found my comfort in it, almost to a fault. The rain hits hard, but the drops seem spread out, not a very driving rain and it's not too cold yet, so it's getting a little warm here in my suit. I would open the suit up but I have learned the hard way; as all good things in my life have been learned the hard way that, if I unzip my suit a little to let some cool fresh air in, the suit will try to rip off of me and violently strangle me. Of course, the only way to stop the suit from strangling me is to pull over, stop and re-fasten it all. It's really not the suit's fault for this, it just has no were for the mass amounts of air flow at 80 m.p.h. to go which, is probably a good thing really. If this suit had open flaps in the back, it would not be so waterproof. Also, I suspect if I opened the suit in the rain that I would get wet or at least my chest would. Then the water would be chilled by the wind and eventually, work its way down to my crotch. Yeah, no thanks, my nether regions have endured enough already, I'll just have to deal with the extra warmth for now. I have to hold my smoke almost in my palm to keep the rain off of it but, I figured this trick out a long time ago, damn I just need to quit smoking.

Putting out the smoke I rummage through my tank bag but can't find my small towel. It's hard to see after a while as the rain is increasing, wiping off my face shield with a small terry towel usually works. Crap, I just cannot find it to save my life. I finally sit as far forward on my seat as possible, slowly unzipping my clothing bag in front of me and rummage in there. It's hard to work around the netting and water bottle but after several minutes of wiping my face shield with my glove and hoping to find a shirt, I find my socks. I take the sock out and appropriate it as my new face shield wiping device. Sometimes I just got to fucking improvise.

After half an hour the rain stops, the sky opens up to a pretty blue with grey clouds and beams of sunshine come down. Wow, that was oddly quick but, I am moving fast, apparently faster than that set of clouds dropping the rain. After a few minutes of riding, giving my suit a chance to dry in the wind, I stop on the side of the road, leave my machine running and wiggle out of my suit in a symphony of Velcro ripping and squirming. Basically, the reverse process of putting it on. Vest, earbuds, helmet, and gloves, "Go Bob, GO!"

Primus "American Life" *Sailing the Seas of Cheese,* Interscope Records, 1991.

These are the moments in life longed for, the beautiful country and wonderful early summer after the rain smells with a nice road and a steady rhythm of moving forward and soaking it all in astride my skoot. I start to gnaw on the beef jerky pulled from my tank bag and take my time with it, enjoying every bit, nice and slowly. I even post another picture of the mountain green road behind me with a cut of jerky hanging out of my mouth. Some of my followers and family are really concerned with how I will eat. So there ya go everybody, I'm eatin'. Thanks for worrying about the subject everybody, but I am 250 pounds of all-American fed man. I am sure I could live for weeks off the extra fat I carry around.

Bob Marshall

My clutch felt a little shy, or almost slipping on my last take off, so I need to adjust it manually at the lever with my left hand. 1 or 2 quarter turns would solve the issue. I guess I could wait till I am stopped to fix this but, when I stop, I just have too many other items to deal with and tend to forget about these small details. Yeah, I can fix this now while thinking about it. Humm, I can't seem to get this adjuster attached to my clutch perch to move. I try a few different angles and fingers but, my hands with my gloves are just not working and the wet of the rain isn't helping much either. Reaching down and slowly maneuvering my left hand in my side saddle bag under my seat, I pull up the tool and go to use it. It's the wrong tool. I pulled a cool Philips #2 screwdriver from the bag but, I need a flat head. I stow the Philips in my tank bag in hopes of not making the same mistake twice. This time I remove my left glove, stowing it in my crotch under my leg. Pass a big rig in the left lane and rummage in my saddle bag again and bam, feel what I am looking for, pulling it out slowly. With the aid of the end of this screwdriver, I get the adjuster or really, the securing nut of the adjuster for my clutch cable on its perch loose and adjust as needed. Then one at time the screwdrivers slowly go back into the saddle bag and the bag, gets lashed close with a belt system I made for it. Must do my best to keep my clutch tight so it does not slip causing premature wear. I have the most expensive clutch plates and springs money can buy, but still, every ounce of preventive maintenance adds the fuck up. And now ya know why I keep all my tools right under my seat, mostly on the left, where they can be reached, while spare parts and sockets go in the right.

In this beautiful and now sunny weather, it's time to apply some more sunblock to my fair white skin. This is done by removing my left glove again, and stowing it in my crotch, rummaging around in my tank bag, finding the sunblock. Removing the cap with my mouth and squeezing a little on my cheeks and nose, I screw the cap back on, still in my mouth, then put the small tube back into my tank bag. Now I can kind of smear it around my face, neck, and nose slowly and get it to cover and soak in my fair face. Yes, all this takes me like 10 minutes but it's not like I have got much else to do while enjoying this scenery, this beautiful sky and operating this hard riding rigid machine between my legs. As I pass slower moving vehicles and big rigs it must look ridiculous to all around me in their cages.

Bob Dylan, "Girl from the North Country Fair." *Nashville Skyline,* Columbia Records, 1969.

Sometimes I can forget it is a rigid frame skoot on this beautiful pavement until there is a pothole or bump and BAM! Sucker punch right to the kidneys and lower back and maybe a knee if I have my legs positioned in a lazy manner. I make it a point to move my position and posture every 15 minutes or so. I can put my foot forward, or back, or in the middle. If I am really desperate, I can even set my feet on a set of pegs I have up on the crash bars, but I rarely do this as it causes me to lean back and sit on my tailbone. It's just how I designed and mounted the seat to sit. More like a flat park bench than an easy chair. I do have some bicycle frame shocks and parts of an old fork spring I cut up and mounted between the frame and the seat. It helps in keeping the sucker punches down. But above all, I have the seat foam cut out where my tailbone sits. I learned a long time ago that I have this oversized back and my tailbone extends lower than most people's do. The solution was cutting a hole in the foam of my skoots seat, it works. No one ever sees it or notices it, as it's under the pleather seat covering but it makes all the difference in the world to me. I do it to all my skoots as I have a few handfuls of them back at home, but my real secret is my saddle rag.

Bob Marshall

My saddle rag is my one true bum saver. I stole the idea from the old American West and the herdsmen or as some entitle them, cowboys, who used them between themselves and their horse's saddle, but you won't see that un-cool factor in the old west movies. Mine originally started off life as a Mexican or south American blanket, the kind they seem to sell anywhere, but this one has been with me for many years and is well worn in and pretty damn soft. I have used it to sleep on, sleep under, sleep around and as a pillow. It even caught on fire once, but it is all mine and I love every square inch of it all beat up, red, black and white. Yes, my butt still hurts after a day or two of good seat time, but every time I stop, it gets refolded and repositioned. I fold it in thirds, in half, in quarters and always moving it forward or back. It's like sitting in a new seat every time I refuel. My big secret of success = my saddle rag.

#10

Goodbye Utah, and welcome to Colorful Colorado. It's not even dinner time yet and I've gotten through a few states. There will be no stopping for dinner tonight. Years ago, when my Pops and I traveled this way on our big Honda cruisers, we stopped for the night around Beaver, Utah. Yeah, moving a lot faster this time, although riding with my Pops behind me is always pretty freakin' sweet, no matter how much he likes to stop and sample the local cuisine everywhere we ride.

The road curves out over a ridge. I can see another storm system ahead of me, I mean like I can see all of it. I guess every state will have a way of welcoming me so 'Welcome to Colorful Colorado Bob!' I scratch my helmet for a minute. Well crap. I pull over to put on my suit again. I ride through the rain, and in a half hour it ends. Okay, maybe next time I will just get wet, this putting on and taking off of the suit is starting to bother me. Not the action, but the time It just takes time and I don't think I have that kind of time, or at least it's debatable because after all, race.

Tang Special, "After the Sunrise" *Bootlegs from Back to the Grind,* Bob Marshall Tape Collection, 1997.

I pull over again, a little frustrated, but dry. The suit comes off and gets re-packed. This road is mine. I'm eating up the miles. Hello Grand Junction and some of the prettiest highway this country has to offer, I am sure. It seems they are doing a bit of road work on the east side of the town, so things slow for a minute over a bridge. Surrounded by big rigs and large family cars, passing safely and extremely slow. Well, this sucks but if I get through it without a scratch or inpatient car running me over, it's a good day. A group of 3 competitors pass me again, all moving fast as hell on their newer Harley Baggers. Wait what? I know I saw these folks at the starting line but how did their skoots qualify for the race? I suspect maybe one or two of them are racing and the other one is what, along for the ride? I'm sure Charlie has some deal with them, and good for them for showing up. Honestly, they all look like they are out for a Sunday cruise, 2 middle aged men and a good-looking woman. I suspect they will pass me several times.

I stop for fuel again at the bottom of the great Colorado Rockies. I remember stopping at this fuel station with my Pops years ago. I fuel quickly and do my routine and even manage to stop for a minute and text Ella who texts me back; she is fine and got home okay. Well shit, I call her, she answers on the second ring. We chat for a few minutes; I tell her where I am and that I am feeling good. Ella can't believe I am moving so fast, she tells me about breakfast with my family and all the good things, but she still seems a little off, like something has put her in a surprised mood. Well, if it was important, she would tell me, I guess. I tell her bye for now and that I will talk to her later. She reminds me how sexy I am, etc. Yeah, the perfect pick me up conversation I needed right about now as the mighty Rockies await.

It's hot and humid where I am, looking up to those great mountains of the Rockies. But I know it will be cold up there, so I put on my Dickies jacket under the vest and endure the swelter of my sticky sweat for now. This jacket is a dark blue poly cotton blend, complete with some cool land speed patches. Not a terribly heavy jacket but, just enough to keep a cool edge off. I figured when it's cold enough for a big jacket, I will just put my suit on keeping my top and bottom warm. The lighter jacket made sense to me during the 10 minutes I spent packing for this trip. Off I go, ready to conquer the Rockies via my skoot and my skoot is happy to be at these high altitudes and running above my expectations.

Nickel Creek, "The Lighthouse's Tale." *Nickel Creek,* Sugar Hill, 2001.

Back on the highway now moving along, and smack into a one lane construction zone behind a FedEx truck doing 35 m.p.h. in a 50-m.p.h. construction zone, SHIT!!! REALLY!?! Well, I won't be blowing my engine up and I sure do appreciate all the packages these people bring, but crap, seriously? Well, I just have to let people be people. I mean the driver is not doing anything dangerous, illegal, to go so slow; the line of traffic behind me feels the same annoyance about the situation as they are all trying to drive up my arse. After several miles the road opens up again and I pass the truck and up through the mountains.

After a few miles, a competitor by the name of Jay is fast on my tail and catches up with me on his older Harley shovel chopper of a skoot. He passes me on the climb where I wave the Stampede wave to him then I fly by him. My engine wants to rev and his wants to torque. Through the Rockies we fly, shuffling positions with a few funny and entertaining antics until eventually I fly far past him enjoying all the beautiful scenery with a little healthy competition.

Coming down the back side, or east side of the mountain range, it starts to get cold. I have to fight the urge to cover up and that works for a little while, but the sun is going down and damn it's getting really, REALLY COLD. If I can just get into Denver for the next stop I can change there, I think. SHIT, I am sure this is way too cold for the human body. I mean my freakin' teeth are chattering. Before a tunnel, I pull over next to a gravel pile on a small shoulder, adorning my sweater under my jacket, heavy gloves and turtleneck while violently shivering and cursing myself for making the wrong decision in waiting so long as the big rigs fly by. Damn it gets cold here quick in these Rocky

Mountains. Also, my face shield is really showing all its scratches as the sun goes down taillights, and especially headlights, are really becoming a problem as they splash streaks of light across my vision. They look as tall as my face shield, sometimes it's hard to make out a car coming at me in the opposing lane or alien spaceships as they appear now.

I pull into Denver just in time for a little post rush hour traffic. The highway is stopped. Oh wait; I am on a cop bike and, from California. I have a few flashing red and yellow lights on my skoot left over from its heyday. With a flip of a switch they come on and I start splitting lanes like I own the road. Within a mile I pass a competitor and yell at him to get behind me. He is shivering and frozen and says he doesn't know how to split lanes. I tell him it's easy and he can follow me. He follows for about a mile then disappears back into stopped traffic. I pass another competitor, stop and yell for him to get behind me. He shakes his head no thanks. What the hell is wrong with these guys? Oh well, I keep skootin' along at a nice 20 miles an hour in the dead stopped traffic with lights a flashing.

A few cars try to cut or nose in front of me, see my flashing lights but it's too late in stopped traffic. One even manages to hit my rear cage as it drags off their front fender. Bummer. That might leave some damage for them. Kind of stupid on their part. I wonder what is going on in these people's minds. Like their rage or jealousy is so great they are happy to endanger my life to make themselves feel better about being stuck in traffic. There seems to be a few of them in every crowd, people who would rather be dead and right than alive and not always right. Well, I have to not let bad or dangerous drivers upset my ride, my Zen on this road is just worth more than that. Finally, all the stopped traffic lets up after many miles and off we all go. Wow that felt like the 91 freeway back home in Riverside for a while there, only Californians take pride in moving over a little as needed to share lanes with us skoot types, that statement is not so true here in Colorado.

Another stop, this time with my suit on. I know I look like a black stay puff marshmallow man wearing a leather riding vest, but I find a big truck stop east of Denver. I notice my lenses for my emergency flashers have fallen off. That construction road in the Rockies must have been tougher than I thought, and the lights are not working. The bulbs have burned out, or in this case, rattled apart. This whole no shocks in the back of the machine thing can really do some damage to these old-style bulbs. I buy a 10 pack of 1157 bulbs and some red lens repair tape at the truck stop, replace the bulbs and wrap the lens frame in tape. Some competitors pull in next to me, I ask them if they picked up my lenses, they both laugh and shake their heads; no luck. Well, lens tape should work for another 2000 miles, Stampede Approved.

Back on the road, into the dark night of Eastern Colorado. It's really dark out here, and really flat. After we got our route last night, my Pops told me he was a little worried about me falling asleep on this section of road. This land was flat and the road straight, not worth much and had to be given to Colorado back in the day. Yeah, it's flat and straight all right with very little traffic, I am sure it is beautiful during the day. As planned, my main headlight is no laughing matter. It's a huge 9 incher bucket with a big blue daylight lamp and a side light to boot. It lights up the night like the 4th of July and, has got to be the best 100 bucks I ever spent at an old Harley store in town called 'Bikers Alley.' Being as I only own one old Harley shovel these days it's not a place I get to visit often, but they have some cool old parts. So, I went in one day looking around a few years back and the owner Bob asked how my cross-country racer build was going? I told him I still needed a headlight, he sat me down, opened a catalogue and said, "Look man, THIS is what you want for what you are doing!" I agreed, gave him the cash and he ordered it for me. My favorite part was building the mount for it. A long 6-inch by 4-inch by quarter inch piece of strap metal. I needed a big American fine thread bolt for it and found, amongst my collection of hardware, just the bolt I needed in my pop's old Harley parts box. I cleaned it up, chased the threads and it was good to go, all old chrome, rustic shiny. I'm usually not one for nostalgia as nothing is truly sacred in the world of racing but, having a little piece of my Pop's old chopper on my chopper is kind of cool.

Yes, my Pops was an old chopper guy. He had a 1959 old cop bike himself back in the day. It was a Pan turned shovel with a racked front springer and a tiny little front wheel, no fender or brake. Complete with a laid-back sissy bar and laid-back handlebars, as a little dude I thought it was the coolest. One of my earliest memories was helping him push it over the oil hole in the backyard. Yeah back in the day dudes just put used motor oil in holes in the ground. Later I would learn that he simply learned this action from an old Boys Life Magazine article, wow times have changed. I remember asking him why the cops ride such funny looking bikes. They were short, and fat looking. "Because they are riding Japanese Kawasaki's and not Harleys," he would proclaim. I did not understand what that meant then, but I do now. A regular factory off the showroom floor skoot looked odd to me when I was a little dude because it looked nothing like my Pops chopped skoot. Also, the rider did not bounce like my Pops did while riding it because it had shocks and my pop's rigid, did not. Oh, the funny things we remember from our childhood regarding our very human parents. So here I am, racing on an old moto patrol chopped Kawasaki across this beautiful, currently dark country. I set my cruise control to rub my eyes then, DEER!

There are only two things that cross-country chopper racers like me really fear: falling asleep behind the bars, and deer. On the straightest of straight roads with my high beam on, I see a field of corn or some kind of tall stalk plant to my right and out of the middle of this, a head Pops out with 2 red eyes about 5 feet off the ground. Throwing myself forward and grabbing my clutch while stomping on the brakes just as this deer turns around and heads back into the tall stalks of the field. Wow, what a fucking eye opener. I breath heavy and start to thank the universe for allowing that situation to go so well. I am scared and can feel myself shaking, I downshift into forth, twist the throttle and back to fifth gear, I also reach forward and turn my big spotlight on. I have to lean way forward to maneuver it but, it's doable on a long straight flat highway such as this. I point it over to the weeds on the right and keep my high beam on, I light up the night and slow to about 70 m.p.h. Yeah, that was the true definition of some fucked up shit, checking my shorts again for the second time today.

Still moving forward with cold calm weather I'm wide awake waiting for the next deer to scare the crap out of me. I spot something odd out of my left peripheral vision. I look down and my phone is lighting up. I hit the screen and a visual of Ella appears. I can see she is in her bed, with her grey sheets wrapped around her and a picture on Marilyn Monroe mounted on the wall behind her. I get all excited and start talking. Then I realize by the look on her face she can't see me, like at all, or even hear me for that matter. I turn on a small flashlight I have dangling off my handlebars and shine it in my face and can see her face lights up to see me. Okay, this is going to be different. I never thought she would video call me on the road. How the heck am

I even getting service out here? I motion with a finger for her to hang on and she nods in approval. I unplug my ear buds from my mp3 player, fiddle with the zipper on the phone case and plug her in and yell into the mic piece, "Can you hear me now?" yelling into my face shield.

"Yes." I think she replies with a smile as she nods in approval and blows me kisses.

I started watching the road again, holding my hand covering and talking into the mic, I give her the updates about the rain, the cold Rockies, traffic in Denver, and deer. She nods as if she hears me, but I can barely hear her or make out what she is saying.

"You are soooo handsome, I am soooo proud of you and how fast you are going!" I finally hear her yell at me.

I thank her and return similar compliments with a smile. She looks so good lying down in that bed of hers. Damn I start thinking to myself, what am I doing out here on this road when I could be home with all of that yumminess? After a few minutes, she flashes me a nipple from her loose nightgown, lifts it up, caressing it with her tongue, and blows a kiss or 3 at me. She waves and I wave back, and we say our goodbyes and goodnights, only I am certain she can't hear me as I really can't hear her, but whatever. The phone shuts off and goes dark. Pulling a smoke from my vest pocket, yeah, I keep a pack in there as well, I hit the lighter. I have a race to run, out here in the middle of the eastern state of Colorado I can't get all homesick for a girl I have only been dating a few months. Yes, she is a sexy one; well-built with all the physical attributes a man could ever desire but racing, is racing. Her large breasts, beautiful face, long dark hair and legs that go for days.

Bob Marshall

Life can be a funny thing for a man like me in my race mode. There is just no sexual desire and no way to feel sexual thoughts, but damn I want to. Even if I got a little tingly, I would not be able to feel it on the skoot here. My body just won't allow it. The turbulence of a rigid frame with the rhythm of the road all equal one big mess devoid of sexual feeling. I have always been a man who needs a lot of stimulation to get hard and sexually excited anyways compared to most I have been told. The woman who I have been blessed with in my life, have had to be very good sports and enjoy the road to sexually exciting me much more than the destination if you know what I mean. I remember being a younger man, in my sexual prime, and for a few women I dated this was just way too much for them. They would get terrible frustrated with how long I took to finish, or I would simply wear them out to the point of exhaustion, and they would run for the hills. Good to be rid of them and those shallow attitudes, but at the time I was sure it was me and not them. I know now it was them. Shallow women who did not know how to please a man like me. The universe always has a funny way of blessing us with good things through bad situations.

As I stated before, Ella was a virgin when I met her. She had no previous sexual experiences to compare me to, so for her sex is a wonderful new experience. The fact it takes some time for us both, is all the more fun. She and I just go to bed early and fall asleep late every night, it works out well.

Lynyrd Skynyrd "Simple Man" *Pronounced Leh-nerd Skin-nerd,* MCA Records, 1973

When we started dating, of course I told F Bomb about her. He was hesitant to congratulate me on dating such a young woman. F Bomb, being 10 years my senior. has been through a lot more in life than most people ever would dream possible and some of it is very dark. I have watched him raise up from the most terrible situations imaginable and stand on top complete and victorious. When he speaks, I listen. After confiding in him that Ella was a virgin, his comments were very to the point. "Bob, that's a young man's game! I mean I know you can handle it I am sure but why do you want to get in a real relationship with this young woman? It's a young man's game that will leave you broken hearted if you let it! Don't make me worry about you, you are my friend and I don't want to see this chew you up. Take your time and just have some fun with her but don't get too serious about it."

I would contemplate his words and feelings on the matter many, many times. What he has stated is very good medicine. I have done my best the last several months to do so. When Ella wants to just stop by to say hi, I inform her my son and I are busy doing something and maybe she could stop by later. Or she would ask if we could go out on a certain night? I state yes, then make her dinner at my house that evening just to make sure she is not out looking for a sugar daddy to take her out all the time. Maybe I am purposely, or accidentally, 10 minutes late to picking her up and I see how that unfolds for her. It turned out it still took her an additional 10 minutes to get ready anyways. I work around my son's schedule as to not confuse him with why she is hanging around us so much. It all worked for a little while, enough maybe to reassure myself it can be said and done, but only for a little while. I have to laugh at myself and my meager efforts. She wanted into my life, into our lives and after a few months of courting her I had to let her in and embrace all the goodness she offered and brought with her.

After my wife left several years prior to this, and after a long drawn out divorce that seemed to go on forever, I always had a great fear that I would meet a woman just looking for a meal ticket. It would all be okay to have this young wonderful woman around to enjoy life with and all we could do together and for each other and she did some good domestic work around the house, and wow she could cook. I am not one to have someone around just to cook or clean or anything like that, but someone who can cook and clean as I do and keep up with me is a huge plus. Having her long legs and large breasts to cuddle with don't hurt me none either.

The road seems to be getting darker and darker now, I am sure it is not, but it has to be 2 in the morning here somewhere in Kansas. I pull off for fuel again, same routine, and maybe some small sugar donuts to assist me in going all night long. Slowly I will eat them in hope the sugar and fresh coffee assist my goal of not dying. I put on my toke or beanie and my turtleneck wrap as well with my big heavy leather gloves complete with gauntlets. I make sure all is secure and tight and it's back on the road.

Rob Zombie, "More Human than the Human" *Zombie Live,* Geffen Records, 2007.

The weather is clear but getting cooler, not cold, just cooler. However, with no windshield or window to roll up and heater to switch on. it is going to slowly creep in. After another hour or two, I can feel it doing just that. It does assist me in staying awake and alert for now. This road is pretty empty on this very early Monday morning. Eventually I lift the face shield for several minutes to keep the cold on my face and my eyes wide open. Slowly working through my trail mix, candies and cigarettes, I know I am in Kansas, but I didn't notice the welcome sign. It all looks the same. I started to see new mile markers counting down the numbers on the side of the road which eventually hit my brain and told me I was in a different state now.

This is where shit gets real, and real dangerous. At what point do I stop, or decide to push on through it all and keep going? Hitting the pavement at this speed in the dark would surely wake me the fuck up, landing me in a hospital or a morgue. The desire to lay down is very real, and very much the problem. Or maybe the solution. I am starting to wander in the lanes, unable to really control my skoot. This is getting dangerous and stupid. Eventually I just can't take it anymore. It is around 4 or 5 a.m. I see a nice-looking rest stop ahead and have to make a decision. It's time to sleep. I am pulling over, right into a damn pajama party.

#11

    Pulling off that tiresome interstate, into a rest stop only to find 4 or 5 other competitors already asleep here. Their bikes are parked near each other, all laid out in strange ways. One is asleep next to his bike lying parallel to it while another is perpendicular. One is just asleep on top his bike. I switch off my engine and creep up hill to the first parking spot available, several spots from the others. I have to push a little to get there - damn my coasting uphill judgement really just sucks right now, I am sure my tired body and current mindset have something to do with that.

    I creep off my skoot, quietly walking far around the bunch of them, off the sidewalk and in the grass too quiet my boots. Up to the restrooms to pee and wash my hands. I manage to see something odd on my way back from the restrooms, an older 60 something year old gentleman who I know has competed in events like this before is sitting upright between his skoot and the curb. I stop and do a double take. He parked his old Harley almost parallel to the curb than, sat on the curb and has is head with his helmet on resting against the front of the frame with one arm up on the front tire. He looks quite comfortable as he snores away but wow, never in a million years would I of thought to sleep against a skoot in such a manner. These old guys sure can teach all of us a few things if we just open our eyes and ears once in a while.

I walk or stumble back to my skoot equally as quiet as before only to notice, I have left my phone on and attached to my handlebars for all the world to see. Humm; do many thieves hang around rest stops in Kansas on a Monday morning and if they do, would they approach a motley looking crew like us? I unzip it from the case on the bars, reply to a few messages, check a few comments on my posts and send a message to Ella letting her know I am somewhere in Kansas, I think and stopping for the night. I lay down next to my hot and dirty moto cop friend who has been so good to me today. With all my gear on including my suit and helmet, I am just too worn out to think about anything but sleep. Propping my boots up on the left pedal board, I cross my legs, cross my arms and close my tired eyes.

With how much I was just falling asleep on the road and fighting not to sway back and forth in the lane I am sure sleep will come easily; it does not. The anxiety from being in a race like this can eat you alive if you let it. The anxiety from being stopped and not moving or making forward progress is slowly but surely working its way into my body's desire to just sleep. Fighting the demons in my brain, I remind myself I am a seasoned runner in this race, there is just no reason for me to get so stupidly anxious about any of it. I lay there for several minutes before I truly find comfort on the hard ground and start to doze off a little. I must admit to myself I am anxious about being stopped but I have to be okay with it. It's healthy for my machine to rest for a few hours and refresh, Okay, maybe that's not entirely true. This bad arse machine has proven itself several times before, it likes to go and really does not need to stop as I have rebuilt it to do so, but telling my brain it's okay for the machine to stop will hopefully work for now.

Every small noise, every large car, I can hear and feel as it vibrates from the highway just 100 feet away, almost calling to me as it all tries to startle me awake. The other loud gnarly dudes sleeping several feet away with all their snoring does not help either; crap! I turn my music on as my earbuds are still in my ears.

John Prine "Angel from Montgomery" John *Prine* Atlantic Records, 1971.

I see something, slowly but surely it all comes into focus from my haze. I see Ella; naked sitting up in front of me on her knees at my feet while I lay in bed. She's smiling, in all the ways she can for me while speaking in that slow sexy voice that drives me crazy. One of our girlfriends is with her as well, also naked and propped up on her knees next to Ella. They are both looking at me with their black hair flowing down their soft warm bodies, kissing and fondling each other. Slowly, they crawl their way up the bed, together. They start kissing me - all of me, slowly and deliberately. Ella spreads her legs over my face, her moisture invades and fills every sense I own. She continues to make out with our third as I fondle and enjoy every soft square inch of them with my hands. The third is slowly riding and grinding my leg, leaving behind a hot, wet trail as only a woman can. Their sounds are becoming increasingly intoxicating as I feel them both reach between my legs. One spits while the other licks and all I can hear is them moaning in unison. In my current position I do not even know which woman is doing what and that only adds to the excitement for me.

My eyes open wide and I jump. I stop, look around into the darkness, hear the road and know it was all a damn dream; a memory. My warm neck turtle has pulled up somehow above my nose, I can feel my warm wet breath on it and its soft texture. One of my legs has fallen off the pedal board and is shoved under the skoot against the warm exhaust pipe. What the hell is going on here and how the hell am I having a sex dream in the middle of a fucking chopper race?!? FUCK!!!

Go Bob, GO! Yeah, that was a wonderful memory and, terrible inappropriate giving the current task at hand. Above all, now I have a minor case of cock ache and neither Ella nor one of our girlfriends is here to assist with that. I jump around and shake it off, wiping my face with my hands and looking around to make sure no one is staring at me. Yeah okay, everyone is asleep. I do see a competitor with a Scooby Doo themed skoot with a mini keg on the back for a spare fuel cell. He has pulled up and parked right next to me and someone else has parked next to him. I wonder for a moment why they parked so close to me; do they think this some kind of pajama party? I have to believe their motive is safety in numbers and also, when I wake up, I will wake them when I fire up my skoot. One hell of a pajama party this is turning out to be; dammit! It's time to move again.

I throw my hand to my crotch and tuck my cock up to my belly button. I then rummage around my front bag and get my dopp kit, very quietly. Stumbling to the restroom, I am reminded of my dream, with every step I take. Brush my teeth, apply more baby powder to the important regions like my pits, chest and my aching cock and even wash my face and hands. I wake up to greet the day and figure by my last known look at my phone, I have been asleep for about an hour and a half. Okay; not as much sleep as I really wanted but it will have to do.

I walk back to my righteous cop skoot gleaming in the parking lot lights. Quietly, everything gets put back in its place on the skoot and I get ready to ride. Slowly, I mount, lean the bike, kick up the kickstand, pull in the clutch and cost backwards. The off ramp for this rest stop is downhill. I back the skoot up so it faces against the arrow on the ground and start coasting downhill to the off ramp. I am going the wrong way but there is no traffic coming at me at 5 in the morning, as I get to the bottom of the off ramp, I turn the key and start the skoot. Making a right turn, I turn the skoot around and it's back to the road, accelerating as slowly and quietly as I can. I think what I just did is, succeed in leaving the rest stop without waking up any of my competitors. I simply slipped away quietly. Those guys are gonna be a little pissed at me when they wake up hours from now and, hours behind me. Go Bob Go!

Dave Mathews Band, "Two Steps." *Crash,* RCA, 1997

The sky is slowly turning a lighter hue of morning gold, that beautiful color that only a June morning can provide, and I get to ride east right into it, right into this beautiful sunrise on this beautiful day; what a treat for me. Kansas is beautiful and the road is straight, wide open and feels like it's all mine. I push in my cigarette lighter, find my smokes in the tank bag and light up. Someday Mr. Marshall; someday soon you are going to quit this nasty habit as eventually, it will slow ya down if you let it. Slurping and enjoying my lukewarm morning coffee, with my morning smoke all at 80 mph, life is good.

I see a few truck stops and gas stations out here on these plains, scattered with no real towns attached to them. I figure they must just have water here or maybe the towns are a few miles off the interstate? I always wondered who lives out here amongst these beautiful green fields and prairie lands. I can imagine their family lineage in this area and these farming interests runs deep, this is when I wish I could stop. Just stop, knock on the doors of these farmhouses and say: "HI! I'm Bob". Nah, my suit and vest might scare them.

Back when I was 19, I got offered a job up the Northwoods of Wisconsin working on a Christmas tree and ginseng farm. Yes, that's right, hundreds of acres of big beautiful balsam Christmas trees and maybe 10 acres of ginseng plants. The owners of the farm had a daughter out in California who had married a friend of mine. I got to do a little of everything out there on this nontraditional farm, even the hard stuff like waking up early with the rest of the family with Mom yelling down into my basement room to get me up. I mostly cut grass between the trees on a 4-foot-wide riding tractor. I also learned to take great care of ginseng. Wow, that was a temperamental plant. Tightening the field covers, trimming the wild trees, weeding, spraying, fixing, welding, maintaining, you name it; I got to do it and even screwed a few things up. The family I lived with there were wonderfully accepting of me even with the few mistakes I made, I learned a lot about family from them. Also care for the land, for yourself, for the equipment and so much more from those 3 months I spent working and earning. Sure a few neighboring farmers chased me away from their daughters while others did the opposite and asked me if I could take their daughters back to California. In the end; I took none with me and left no offspring that I know of. To this day; I use a lot taken away from that experience. I may live back in a big city now, in my little old house attached to a small public street but, I remember what it's like to live in the middle of nowhere, and I loved every minute of it.

Maybe one day when I decide to grow up a little, I can have some land somewhere in the middle of nowhere. Run solar and wind power off the grid, raise my own crops and harvest my own fuel from the land. Maybe trade for what I need, be out of the laws of society, a true American Outlaw. Just someone who simply does for themselves, with what they have invested their time and sweat into. Oh sure, I would still get to pay taxes on my land and road registrations for my skoots and stuff like that so, I would still need some type of dollar income but, the more I do for self, the farther I am out of the matrix. If I can grow most of my own food, raise my own meat rabbits and chickens, use true horsepower and not pay taxes on petrol fuel or maybe use an alternative like, gasification: that would be on hell of a living.

Gasification sounds complicated to most but it's really not. If you have enough wood on your land and a little mechanical smarts, you can build a gasification generator. Yes, it's basically a large smudge pot and you attach the exhaust to the intake of the engine. If you get the stoichiometry, or fuel to air mixture right, it will burn and run all day long.

Maybe a large solar panel array built 12 feet in the air that I park my skoots under for shade and, with some smart technology my Pops mastered a few years ago, the array slowly follows the sun allowing greater solar energy to be collected; now that would be cool. Maybe a few wind turbines as well. Hook it to a converter, and a smart voltage regulator with a small shed full of good ole golf cart batteries and bam: I am an electrical generating power plant. More importantly I am MY VERY OWN electrical generating power plant. I would get to maintain it and keep it going but once set up and running, I would owe no man for the power it creates for me. I reckon as long as I don't have 20 hair dryers going at the same time or have to run a welder all day; I should be okay.

My other favorite has always been hydrogen. If there is enough electricity, I can split the atoms of common water and make hydrogen and it will really explode. With that electrolysis I could run any internal combustion engine, I just need a lot of amperage to do it. If I had the solar already, and it's a bright hot day, I might as well run a generator or even an old farm truck or tractor off a portable electrolysis set up.

My point is: it can be done, with very little if not any loss to modern convenience. For so long now we have relied on petrol fuel and electrical power plants to do for us and keep us paying them for what energy we think we need. Imagine a man or woman or family working their own power, living off their own land and not paying the man. Those people are the true American Outlaws. The true Americans who say: "thanks for the offer Mr. Big Corporation but I will be doing my business elsewhere, and by elsewhere, I mean, myself". I hope to get close to this image of the American Outlaw when I grow up.

So, who opens a truck stop out here anyways? Well they seem busy as I can see them for miles before I get to them because there is nothing obstructing my view in this flat land. Just pretty green grasses and big petrol stations.

Judy Collins, "My Father." *Who Knows Where The Time Goes.* Elektra, 1968.

I start to stretch and get ready for the day both physically and mentally. Some arm stretches, some leg stretches, some back movement and shoulder rolls all while using the wind as resistance. Can anyone guess what I will be doing all day? If I get lucky and keep my head on straight, the answer is: running east in this race. Riding and navigating this rigid chopped skoot - all day long. I lean forward on the handlebars and prop my feet back on the passenger pegs. It's not terribly comfortable but it allows me to lay on my forearms in a different than usual position for a while. I start to realize as the light is getting brighter in the sky that the sun is rising on the road almost directly in front of me, I am riding right into it. I speed up a little in anticipation. I must be doing close to 100 m.p.h. now stretch out almost on top of the bike, feeling fast and confident in the anticipation of the rising sun then; nothing.

Just like that, I feel the inertia of the bike slowing down and push me forward. I look down and realize I don't feel or hear my engine anymore. I quickly jump and re-position myself to my usually scheduled program. I pull the clutch and hit the start button, but nothing happens. I find neutral then reach down to fiddle with the key and nothing. My skoot is dead and not responding, I have to pull over and stop. I do so and realize there is only about 4 feet on the right side of the road of hard shoulder. I look behind me in my rear-view mirror; no vehicle is in the slow lane right now. I take my gloves off and dismount to the right, away from traffic instead of my usual left but yes, I leave my helmet on.

I quickly realize that seem to have no power at all. When I flip the key, the small L.E.D. indicator I wired to the headlight and whipped to the handlebars that showed my voltage is not even on. Okay, must be a fuse; that's weird as I rewired this bike myself years ago. It's really weird because I used to be an electronics technician. I can wire and rewire with the best of them, so this is odd. I built a mount for the blade style car fuses under my seat so I can easily get fuses almost anywhere as needed. I know I carry a few extra so; here I go.

I look behind me into oncoming traffic and see a few scattered big rigs and small family type cars coming at me, but they are few and far between and are merging into the fast lane for me. I open my saddlebags for a few spanner wrenches to unbolt my seat, giving a wave and thumbs up to big rigs and cars as they move over, "Thank you strangers". They wave back, it seems we are all in this together.

I unbolt my seat and flip it almost straight up; I use the bungee cord that usually holds the back of my tank bag down to lash it forward to the handlebars. Yeah, I have done this a few times and some things I carry serve double purpose like, this old black bungee cord. I quickly find the bad 10-amp fuse, it looks like it's for the starting relay but not the main 30-amp fuse, just for the starting system as I have none of them labeled, it's all in my head. I quickly replace it, turn the key, hit the starting switch and the bike fires to life. Humm; must have just been a bad fuse, I guess that's possible but not likely. Re-securing the mountings for the seat, re-stowing tools and miscellaneous parts back in their assigned saddlebags and I am off again; Go Bob, Go!

Rolling now, I merge into traffic and up shift then, comfortably lay back out on the bike. A few miles down the road I pass another big gas stop. Wow, gas stations everywhere, lucky me. Time to get comfortable again, the skoot is skootin'. Five minutes later, I feel the inertia give out and the bike throwing me forward again. Darn; something seems to be really wrong and I need to figure this out, like quick and now.

Same situation but a few miles down the road, all the cars and big rigs I just passed move over for me again. I use this quick moment to take my suit off, stow it and throw my jacket on. I replace the fuse as before, go to hit the start and realize, the start button is gone. All that remains is its small spring. I hit the spring and the bike starts then, an arch at the spring and the skoot dies. Cool; problem found. I pull the small spring out, cut into my right handlebar wiring harness and find the red and black wire for the start button, I cut them out and expose about 25.4 mm of wire on both of them. Another new fuse, seat back down and tools stashed and secure, I wrap one wire around the handlebars. I hold the other wire and connect them, and the bike starts. I quickly separate them as needed. I am moving again, upshifting and getting back into the light traffic on this Monday morning here on the west side of the great plains of Kansas.

I look over and realize this wire is jumping around next to the ground of the handlebars. Setting the cruise control, I reach way back on my left side and grab a roll of electrical tape off of the bungee cord. With how far back it is I really cannot reach it but manage to undo the front of the 30.48 cm bungee cord, slide the tape towards me and bam, it's on my finger. I then manage to re-secure the bungee to a frame gusset as I had it before. Yeah that took like 10 minutes but, I don't have much else to do and I saved myself the several minutes of pulling over and the danger of the narrow shoulder. I pull several centimeters of tape with my teeth and cover the wire, that makes me feel better. I would hate to engage my starter at this speed. I know the starting clutch would not really care but still, the better I can be to my machine, the better it will be to me. I pop the tape into my tank bag in hopes I remember to put it back on its bungee cord dispenser system later.

Wow do I have time to think out here. I slowly text Ella 'good morning' but know she probably won't be up for several hours. I take another picture of myself and post it as it adds my location to the post. I open my jacket a little as the sun has risen which I kind of missed while farting around with that bad starter switch. The sun, our sun is right in front of me, staring me down reminding me; it's going to be a nice long day of riding. Just moving as fast and as efficiently as possible on an hour and a half of sleep. I block that from my mind and take my time reapplying sunscreen.

It may seem like a big deal to stop on the side of the road and fix something to keep moving forward but I must admit, I have some experience in this department. When I was a younger man; I drove a big old white 1966 convertible Cadillac. My Pops bought it from an old lady out of South Central, Los Angeles and I just fell in love with it. For the next several years my weekends were filled with small repairs and projects surrounding that wonderful machine. It needed some new heads which my

Pops and I made long fun work out of. Then it needed upholstery and a new top which my Pops paid to have done but not before we hit a few junkyards and rebuilt all the window motors and a few other fun mechanical items. We stripped all the old cheap paint and putty off of it and sent it to a painter for a new, white, paint job. That took a little longer than expected as the guy worked out of his house in the next town over. But by the time I was 16, it was a rolling machine I drove to high school and far beyond. Needless to say, it was kind of cool cruising around in that land yacht of true Detroit symbol of Americana. I lived in the city of Corona then, next city over from Riverside and attended Corona High School. My best friend: Greg Doyle and I used to load up friends, (mostly girls) and just cruise. The interior of the car was large enough that 4 or 5 people (girls) could fit across the back seat and a few in the center of the front seat. They just had to be okay with Greg and I using them as armrests. Yeah, I got into a little trouble with this fine automobile, hell I even got arrested and thrown in jail once but; nobody died. Sure, it broke down on me a few times, but never really left me on the side of the road. I just kept on wrenching it back to life and kept moving forward.

Within a year of cruising this beast around high school I was dating my daughter's mom. I got to rebuild a cool old car with my Pops and learn to wrench, got laid a lot because of said cool old car, and got a perfect human being of a daughter out of the mix. The universe is just awesome like that sometimes.

.

#12

Riding through this part of the race, my body is starting to groan at me. It groans and moans when I hit a bump or get into a bad patch of road. Other times it's the constant of sitting forward, my back and legs reminding me that I am no longer a spry young man of 20. Hands are going numb but still serving me, no soft mounts on these handlebars so, it's like hanging on to a batter mixer or hand drill; forever. Some of the time I can just ride with one hand and also have the option of setting my crude cruise control, freeing my right hand. Texting on my phone however is out of the question now, my fingers will no longer hit the screen as needed, will have to go old school and just make a call like it's 1999. But there are tricks, let me restate that: I have a ton of tricks for fighting against and working with my body. Slowly but surely, these tricks will be implemented, refined and even invented as needed for the rest of this race. Damn, I hope they work for me and I hope I am clever enough to get this done.

Bruce Springsteen "Born to Run" *Born to Run,* Columbia, 1975

Bob Marshall

When I started riding again seriously after a brief hiatus about 10 years ago; I can remember holding onto the bars for dear life at faster speeds, as if my life depended on it, like I was hanging from a chain link fence. It took me a little time back in the saddle to remember I did not need to hang on THAT much. I mean I don't hang on or death grip that tight to the steering wheels of cars, why would I on my skoots? I believe the answer to this question lies within a deep understanding in our modern America society. A fact none of us can really escape rather we like it or not and that is; we have all grown up riding IN cars.

From our first days of our parents driving us home from the hospital, we all know what a car is and what it feels like to ride in one. How to open the door, slide in, fasten seatbelts and we lean a little or brace ourselves as needed in all the 3D motions of left and right, forward and back, and up and down for the car ride. Have you ever met someone who did not ride in a car until they were much older? I have; he spoke of being raised on a bee farm somewhere in the Midwest and did not ride in a car till he was in his early teens. The car was going at such a fast speed of 30 miles per hour he was sure he was going to die. Moral of it all is, unless you were raised with your parents taking you to Sturgis every year for the big biker rally or to the store and back via skoot; you do not know what it feels like to ride, it is simply not engraved into you as riding in cars is. Oh sure if you can ride a bicycle you can ride a motorcycle but few of us ever venture from the sidewalk or protected bike lanes on bicycles and if we do, it's not at the speed of an internally powered engine of this fine 2 wheeled machine. On a skoot, you are out there, exposed, part of the surroundings and that includes the tonnage of steel of the cars around you, just a few feet in either direction. With no cage for false protection around you or tinted windows to hide behind, everywhere you go, people can see all of you. So the answer is, if all of us got the opportunity to be introduced to riding from birth, we would all be experts at just sitting on skoots and letting the skoots work for us but; we in these fine United States of America do it differently. If anyone wants to ride around here, usually they have to: learn to ride. I mean you learn to ride a bike as a little one usually so why not a bike with an engine built in? It never seems to be that easy for our American lifestyle. You take a class, take a riding test, apply for and receive a special M class license, find a skoot to buy that may or may not fit you. Then, and only then, can you truly see if your dream of rebel folklore skootin' down America's highways will come true.

You will spend hours and hours learning to control the bike as needed in traffic, bad weather, and under all sorts of circumstances and situations that do not usually affect the modern automobile. The passion, want, and drive to ride a skoot has to be great, up there with those of us who get the privilege of commuting to work via skoot or touring around these Americas and even competing in illegal road races like this. Yeah it takes a lot to get to where I am on 2 wheels but totally worth it in my humble opinion. Like anything else in life that is worth doing you just: begin. All the questions you have will farm more questions and eventually you get answers and more answers until you are answering your own questions. All you have to do is begin and enjoy the advance citizenship of skoots.

The one I always hear is that motorcycles are recreational vehicles; what the hell does that even mean? When you insure a motorcycle, you get to insure it as a recreation or second vehicle. If you sign up for a towing service you pay for a car towing package then, motorhome and motorcycle package on top of that. If you break down and have to pay cash for a tow, they will try to charge you extra as if you were a large motorhome or recreational vehicle. I just don't understand how a smaller 2 wheeled vehicle could ever be referred to as recreation anything. You can and will get anywhere cheaper, faster and easier on said 2 wheeled vehicles.

So, what if we took all the young, single, men under 30 for example and gave them motorcycles? The answer is not totally cut and dry, but we would effectively eliminate all of our traffic congestion and not have to build additional lanes for our roads. Imagine all the fun life would be if all our young people simply skooted around. As a society we would all watch out for them, watch over them, and allow them to be young and take up less space on our roadways while still allowing them to get their butts to college and/or out in the workforce. I have a real opinion on this; it's very simple, have fun with whatever you do in life. If you see something you want to do, buy a magazine or research as needed but then simply; begin.

Personally, I was not raised in a family of motorcycle riders. Yes, my Pops rode a lot before he had kids and some after however, the story goes my mother threatened to turn his chopper into a coffee table if he did not sell it. Off it went, sold to the next young man with Americana folklore aspirations of kicking an old rigid Harley around. When we all go through this wonderful thing called life it seems we have a lot of choices to make. Drink this, eat that, smoke this, walk, ride or drive. I drive sometimes when I have got the kids with me in my big arse dad mobiles but when I can, I choose to ride. The wind in my face, money staying in my pocket, get out and feel the weather: ride. It really is advanced citizenship, everywhere I go I get there better, faster, and more economically than the next guy.

My love for 2 wheels started way back when I was 8 and raced BMX bikes with my family race team. Most weekend my dad would load up the old Winnebago motorhome or the

Caprice Classic station wagon and off we would go to the nearby towns of Perris, Norco or Lake Elsinore to have some family fun. A few neighborhood friends, with my older sister and younger brother, jumped in. Even my little sister who had to be like three years old at the time got half a lap on her big wheel with all the other younger siblings. Sure, we had a few good sponsorships, but we weren't all that competitive. We just kind of showed up, enjoyed the races, fought over who was going to be making the sandwiches and what kind of sandwiches to make while wearing our cool racing leathers and pedaling our arses off on the track. It was simply about good family fun, a good life lesson from my Pops to my siblings and myself, how to be a single dad and rock it with a motley crew of children.

I would ride my BMX bike almost everywhere; around the neighborhood, half the town, and for my paper route. It was the mid-1980s so kids could get away with stuff like jumping off curbs and throwing heavy papers at your doorstep at 6 am while not wearing a helmet. But I was simply riding; feeling the wind in my face. When I got older, I naturally wanted to ride motorcycles, I mean 2 wheels that don't need to be pedaled: yes please! I had an old 125 Yamaha my friend's dad, Milton Pasternak, gave to me. I would tool around on it a little in college but had a few issues with it that I did not know exactly how to repair back then. Let's face it, before You Tube or the act of Googling repair manuals was available; it was kind of harder to fix stuff, so fixing stuff, might be out of the question. The old guys could be helpful but damn sometimes they just talked way too much and you rarely got the information out of them you truly needed. In my mid 20s I got married and my wife had no interest in me riding and killing myself on it, so I got rid of it; HUGE MISTAKE!

Bob Marshall

After a few years of being married, my Pops got a used motorcycle; a red 2000 Honda V-twin 1100, water cooled and everything. Yeah, I took one look at that machine and really wanted to ride again. Finally, my Pops and I took a class together and my wife conceded that if I wanted to kill myself on a motorcycle; I was welcome to do so. I know she did her best to be supportive but needless to say, she was just never quite happy with me and motorcycles: hence her title these days is simply 'my son's mom' not 'my wife.'

The biggest problem with the idea of touring on a motorcycle is that it is very foreign, and even scary, for most everyone on this planet. You take a class, take a test, get your license and okay, now what? Some commute, some might ride on the weekends with friends or as part of a riding group but how do you learn how to tour on a skoot, like really ride across this great country on 2 wheels? Imagine how many times I have sat down with people who are either in awe or just disbelief that I tour the way I do and even race a skoot cross country - let alone a personally built jobber like mine that is missing a set of shocks. Some have questions but most are of the opinion that what I and my competitors are doing is just for the 'elite' or 'crazy dumb shit' of a rider. In these conversations I work hard to get them to know that this is my sport; like other people hike, climb, or go bowling. They are usually polite in their amazement or statements of how crazy they think I am but occasionally I get the simple "I don't know how you do that; I could NEVER do that!" statements. This is always a real bummer for me. It has to come from somewhere deep inside the individual making the statement and it REALLY sucks to hear. Sometimes I have caught myself responding with a statement like, "Hey it's okay, don't compare yourself to me, I'm a little sick in the head when it comes to wrenchin', riding, and racing." I am simply using this statement, so they don't walk away thinking that I am an asshole for talking up my riding abilities. I don't view what I do as a direct ability of my riding skill. Yes, I have a lot of skills, but it has come from years of practice and pre thought as to what it takes to get an old hand rebuilt machine across this country in one shot. However; I truly believe anybody who rides can do this. When any of us make the statement that: 'we cannot do it', we have already failed.

Citizen Cope "Son's Gonna Rise" *The Clarence Greenwood Recordings*. RCA Records, 2004.

This road is proving to be fantastic, just totally clear of clutter. The weather is nice, and this morning ride is just what I needed to start day two of my cross-country chopper racing. The green in the rising and falling flat hills around me just puts my mind at ease. I have spent a lot of time and money to get myself here, best to sit back, flex my body and mind and simply enjoy the now, almost distraction free. As young people set out in their lives there is so much distraction - like true commercial distraction. It can really overwhelm so many a human being, so many of us just don't truly get to find what makes us happy. Always someone is trying to sell us a better, more comfortable life and get our hard-earned money. It's too hot, too cold, too rough, too soft, too hard, too old - and on and on. We cannot do this or enjoy that until we buy this product or that product, and we can finance it, simply buy now and pay later. We are always at the mercy of what we give away to have that dream we think will, make us happy. From my personal experience, I can tell ya from my experience that dreams are made from a lot of planning and pre thinking with a side of adventurous attitude and a want for something greater and more self-filling. Let's all get out there and get our giddy on. Let's go enjoy life and make a game out of how little we spend or how little we give to the man in our adventure. This is my game, no matter how good or bad I might be at it, this is the road I choose to run.

Sooner or later on this race I'm gonna have to start figuring out the cold, hard, facts on my life and how to make myself better in the today of my situation with good decisions. Lately it's all piled up on my plate as I have allowed it; shame on me for letting said plate get so damn full. Sooner or later; for now, I am happy to enjoy running here on my road.

This highway system is all set up for us. There are only a few places, mostly in the west where you won't find a gas station every 100 or 50 miles. Rarely can a skoot go more than 150 miles stock so it's okay to add an extra fuel tank. Petrol fuel that we buy at the pump only weighs just over 6 pounds per gallon. If you want to worry about the extra weight, just lose 20 pounds and shut up about it. It's not that big of a deal, add a few gallons, or carry an emergency fuel can. Yes I carry almost 3 extra gallons in my spare fuel cell mounted on the front of my skoot and, just in case things get stupid and I run out or a friend needs fuel; I also carry a stainless steel water tumbler of extra fuel. That thing only holds 14 ounces, just enough to get you started again really, but I don't want to have to stop and refill my fuel, like ever, that exercise would take way too much time. I will be stopping every 220 miles or so to refuel, if I have to turn my petcock under my tank to the main tank reserve I can, but damn that would be bad planning on my part. Easier and faster to stop to refuel when needed and when the road allows and enjoy the now of fuel availability.

Living in the now is always the best road from my personal experience but, totally an exercise of Grecian proportions to get my mind around it sometimes. Today I am healthy, I have air in my lungs, my children are safe, warm and healthy and today my skoot, is moving flawlessly across these 3000 miles of road. There are only 2 types of mechanical devices in this world, those that are broken and those that are going to break. It does me no good to worry when this machine will break, I just have to sit back and enjoy the now of it moving forward from my hard work of repair and preventive maintenance. I have always done my best to put myself in the old school thinking that if ya own it, it's okay to know how to maintain and fix it. Sometimes yeah that means handmade and beaten forged metal parts that aren't so shiny. Hell; sometimes they may not even have a coat of paint on them but my parts work well for me, as I design and build them to. Other times it means hockey stick tape and duct tape but above all of that it means, I did it myself. I did it for me and my machine and it keeps me competitive in this race - so far. Sure, I get flak from the normal consumer on my skoots that I rebuild and ride, I take all that flak as a compliment. I enjoy the lack of education so many people have on what works and what does not, or what is cool and what is not. All that can be said is; until you ride like myself and my competitors, ya don't get to judge a book by its cover. It ain't what's on the outside that counts, and chrome don't get ya home. Wow I can go on and on. Above all, we all get to find our own road, and our own way down that road. Sure, my way looks a little different but I'm moving faster and farther than most in this modern age via old skoot down this road; my road, my way, in the now. To a man like me, that is the current definition of freedom.

I find myself in the east side of Kansas; stopping again for fuel, a big bathroom break, coffee, beef jerky, refill my trail mix container, water, oh look a banana on sale if you buy 2, just like the water oh and maybe some of those little crumbly donuts I only allow myself to enjoy once a day on the road like this. I take a glance at my phone realizing I have not heard from Ella yet today. I call her with no answer, I try to send her a text, but my fingers aren't working; crap... oh well.

I jump back on the skoot, button up and go, accidentally leaving my light jacket on and the humidity of the middle of Kansas is raising. I open it and accept the small discomfort of warm and wet, so I don't have to stop. Soon I see it; a storm system right over the road in front of me and am about to ride into it, of course. If I look close enough, I think I can see the beginning and end of it. It's hot and humid as hell and damn I would hate to put my suit on now. I stow my phone in my tank bag, find my sock to wipe my face shield off, which took like 10 minutes as it was buried in my tank bag, and simply get comfortable in my decision. Well, here goes nothing, time to get pelted and wet. I ride through it, ringing my yellow leather gloves out as I go to keep my grip. It starts light, then gets heavy for 20 minutes but then it is done and back in the humid heat of Kansas on a June day.

I get my phone from the tank bag and can see Ella has responded and even tried to call me back, that was nice of her and puts a big smile on my face. I'll have to catch up with her soon enough. Getting into Kansas City now and just in time for some early lunch hour traffic. Being from a big city myself, this Kansas City traffic won't bother me too much, I think. I have to smile and remember a family vacation many years ago when I was maybe 12 years old. My mother, siblings and I were in this big city and had to get somewhere in the rush hour traffic of the evening. My grandfather was very worried about it but at the time, my mother was commuting from Corona to Anaheim where we lived back in California. Needless to say, the "traffic" we encountered was pretty light and my mother had no issue navigating our rental car though it all in this big city. Compared to the traffic of Southern California, the idea of traffic here was very light and manageable. That was 25 years ago, I suspect it might be the same story today, but I mentally brace myself for anything; anticipating traffic will come to a stop soon enough.

Traffic slows but never stops. I feel my neck and arms being pelted by something, fine B.B. sized dirt maybe? I move from lane to lane hoping to find relief from it but can't escape it. The tires from the cars in front of me are just picking it up and throwing it high enough for me to catch it right in the face. Something is wrong with this road, I need to get in front of this mess and fast, this shit is annoying. Speeding up, swerving through traffic and after a few miles find the source. An old beat up van towing a car trailer has decided that this car trailer, is suitable for hauling dirt. It's just making a mess falling all over the road. I pull next to him and yell to him he needs to secure his dirt, it's making a mess. The older, not so gentlemanly type driver listens to me, then flips me the bird, I smile and wave back.

Reaching into my left tool saddle bag and grab something, anything, I find a smaller or stubby Phillips screwdriver. Calmly I pull in front of him and see pretty clear traffic ahead of me and, accidentally drop the screwdriver in the air with very little movement. Darn; I hate it when that happens but every so often, ya just lose grip of something on a skoot and away it goes into the air. I wonder if I should stop and pick it up? In my rear-view mirror, I watch as the tool slams his windshield with a sharp bang. I can't see if his windshield cracked or not as I quickly shift down a gear and hit the throttle and calmly jam the fuck out of there. He slows as I accelerate with as little fanfare as possible. Eventually I see him pull to the side of the road. Okay; not my finest moment but damn people sometimes, and their crap attitudes towards public roads. Public roads people, we all get to share it, from big rigs to fragile skoots, it's all for public use.

#13

Missouri now, or 'Missura' as I usually hear it from my mom. Flying through the town of Independence, land of my Mother's birth. My grandparents, aunts and their families still live here but, I don't have time to stop and say hi. Any member of these United States has to be amazed while traveling through these parts of the country especially for a wild west born and raised dude such as myself. Over 100 years ago a bunch of people were sold on the idea of westward expansion and how much land and opportunity there was on the west side of this country. They all packed up what they had, got together inexperienced mule teams and wagons and spent many months, from the spring to the fall, to head west with their families in tow and very little experience traveling. It was a migration above any of our comprehension today. These men, women and children with not really knowing what lay in store just began and made it happen. Most had no clue how to drive the teams of beasts they just spent their life savings on, but they made it happen. Starting off from towns like Independence, Missura here just going west on the Oregon Trail, true, badassery. My helmet is off to those true pioneering types, that kind of gumption and moxie is hard to find these days in our human race.

Primus, "Wynona's Big Brown Beaver" *Tales from the Punchbowl*, Interscope, 1995

Stopping for fuel again, same story, different Petrol station and walking around half wet from the last little storm there. Pee, coffee, water, fuel, check oil and add a little, then the skoot and I do a few laps around the gas station parking lot to wax my chain. Spraying under my left leg where there is a clear shot because; no, I do not have on the stock chain guard, I tore that bitch off years ago. Instead I built one that's really just a piece of 1-inch angle iron welded to the frame, parallel with the chain. This action of lazy circles must look really ridiculous to the general surrounding public but guess what; I don't care.

Hitting the open road again and forgetting to remove my jacket again, priorities, I guess. It is doing a good job keeping me from swimming through the air and, for now, that's comforting. Sometimes this humid air can get really sticky and thick, just very hard to move through and it's really felt with no windshield. Opening my cuffs and unzipping the jacket a little bit more seems to get me a little air to my arms and chest. Also, I forgot to call Ella back, maybe next stop.

I feel my clothes dry now and will just take the warmth and fight the fatigue. Feeling good, but I am not exactly sure why. Naturally the adrenaline of running a race like this will keep me going for a while or keep me awake the night before in worry and wonder. I got a good 5 hours of sleep the night before this race at my stepmom's house in Barstow which happened to be right down the street from the Hotel California. Everyone in my family went to bed on time in their own beds in their own rooms. Ella and I made love twice and slept in each other's arms like babies. Then we all woke up and came to the starting line refreshed and ready. I am sure some of my competitors did not sleep at all that night in their anxiety or anticipation for this race and most I am sure did not get laid. I am just having to move a little slower through this humidity, really having to lean into it and the machine is fighting a little hard to keep up.

Why am I not home right now with Ella on her knees in front of me? Hopefully soon enough this heavy humidity will leave me alone, maybe this fighting will become my new normal or comfortable. Yeah, I better get used to it; it is now my norm. I will simply have to operate in it to move forward. Best to shut up about it and take it while accepting I left my hot young girlfriend at the starting line.

The road is smooth and clear, warm and dry for now. I'm passing big rigs often and moving with the fast cars. Did you know yellow leather gloves bleed when they get wet? Yup. I've had yellow hands most of the day now. The gas attendant really noticed at my last stop. Time to ride, I mean really ride; keep riding and then some. I got into listening to audio books lately, what entertainment to have someone read to me. Taking off my left glove, I scroll through my own personal library on my phone I pull up "The Man Who Would Stop at Nothing" by Melissa Holbrook Pierson. Wow, what a great book about the Iron Butt Association and the Man, Rider and Legend; John Ryan. Good motivation for me right about now. I have to listen to every word as Melissa is that writer that writes straight on, with nothing assumed or left between the lines. It is all poetry and I better be paying attention, or I might miss something.

I have got to think to myself, wouldn't it be cool someday to ride like John Ryan? Well, it may not be in the cards and I am okay with that but: WOW, DAMN IT WOULD BE COOL TO RIDE LIKE JOHN RYAN. I don't have to beat any of his records, but just to compete like he did and so many like him and around him. Unfortunately, for all of us he was lost in a motorcycle accident a little while back, riding and doing what he loved to do on 2 wheels. I personally never figured out the exact story but feel the loss as so many of us Road Runner and Racer types did. Ryan did some pretty amazing feats as fast and far as imaginable and beyond, all on 2 wheels. Enjoying the now of this muggy day, I can really think, enjoy, and admire his awesomeness thanks to someone who wrote all about it for the rest of us.

I think - yeah there seems to be another storm coming at me, but I can't see the end of this one. The cars heading towards me are just soaked and the rain starts; time for another fuel stop. As soon as I pull to the pump island under the carport, it starts to pour. I look at my phone but can't really seem to make out which way the storm is heading. Thinking old school in this, it might be easier for me to step inside and find someone coming from the east to tell me about the storm.

As I walk in; I can hear the murmurs all around about the storm and find a man with 3 children sitting at a booth eating at the fast food joint attached to the gas station. I calmly approach him and his table and ask if he just drove through the storm? The table gets quit and yes that includes the kids as he says he has, and it is sheeting down and he had to stop. I thank him and smile as one of the kids asks: "What - are - you?"

The dad shushes him while I smiled and responded; "Oh that's ok: my son is about your age little dude and he thinks, I look like a pirate." 2 of the children laugh a little.

"But I am just riding on a motorcycle kid, it's a good way to get around."

The boy has a questioning look on his face, something like; "It's raining outside weirdo, why are you riding a motorcycle today?" I'll leave it to his dad to explain. I smile and thank him again for the information, step to the counter and order a sandwich.

My mind is in a haze as I sit and watch the rain fall hard. Nervously I stand at a high table and eat, can't even see the skoot anymore which I left under the carport next to the pump. It's not too crowded so I have no guilt in doing this for now. My grip on reality is slowly slipping, the stress on my mind and body is real. This little break should do me some real good in re-centering my sense of reality.

Finishing my sandwich, I walk outside under the cover of the portico, light a smoke and call Ella. This is my first time stopping to eat and smoke, simply a rare treat brought on by the rain. Ella is excited to hear from me and has a lot of questions. I give her all the updates and listen to her questions, trying to answer them gracefully. Mostly she is in awe and not always sure what to ask as this world of racing is totally new to her. I ask her about her day so far, but she does not have much to say as she is playing it off, keeping it distant from me. Oh well, if it's important, she'll tell me about it when she is ready. Instead she goes into great explanation of how proud she is of what I am doing, and she can't believe how fast and far this race is taking me and how she can't wait to get her mouth on my cock. Wow; that woman...for being so young and inexperienced in these items of relationships, she sure does know how to put a smile on my face and my cock. Saying goodbye for now we hang up, yeah, I am getting a little tingle at this point after that conversation but, it's time to get back to the business at hand: racing.

The rain should have let up by now, these summer storms usually come and go no matter how violent they are. I get to the skoot, get my suit on and stow everything as needed. The skoot takes a few tries to start, must be the heavy rain but I manage to coax it back to life and off into the wet, hot day we go. Damn it's hard to even find the freeway onramp. Everything is so wet and green and without curbs I'll most likely slide into a drainage ditch if I'm not careful. I made sure to get a mental map of the on ramp while still standing at the gas station but damn, I am almost blind out here. It's pouring and pounding rain, I just have to find a big rig and put it in front of me. Trust them to see where I am going because the road, has disappeared in the haze of heavy, shin pelting mist.

I take the wrong road and end up on a frontage road, next to a Honda motorcycle dealership. Well that's nice and I am glad they are here, but I don't think I need any motorcycle parts right now, I flip a bitch, very slowly backtracking to the on ramp. That probably looked really ridiculous to the fine people of Honda inside the dealership. What an idiot I must look like to the likes of those dry folks selling side by sides and mowers.

I stop and wait for a moment on the side of the on ramp and see a nice big rig soon moving well in my direction. I hit the gas, jam the gears and get behind them, slowly at about 45 miles per hour. Cars are still passing me in the left lane throwing a wave of water on to me and the skoot. I have open air filters that will try to take on water if I let them so, when a car comes on my left, I have to move or skate to the right side of the right lane behind the big rig then, I move back to the left side of the lane in hopes of being on the top edge of the road. Avoiding the watershed or even worse, a puddle on the right side of this slow lane is my plan for now. The funny trick is, I can't always see the cars passing in the left lane, my mirror is pretty useless in all this wet. Most of the time I hear them as my earbuds are currently out and the wave of water they produce will hit me and my open filters, which will cause the skoot to shutter a little as it tries to burn the water it is intaking with the usual fuel and air. For the most part, my legs guard the air filters and I move my saddle rag forward to assist in this. It's not that big of a deal but something else to keep on my mind to keep me and my skoot moving forward in this downpour of water. Go Bob Go, and: Go Skoot Go!

The rain lightens up eventually after half an hour or so. I can open my suit a little to let some dry air in. Back at the last gas station I was too lazy to put my vest on and with my suit open now, it is choking me and trying to fly off my body in the wind. They just did not design this suit to be worn on a skoot without a windshield and with the front open and honestly, that's okay. I mean if they did it would be made out of leather, not the cool synthetic blend it is. Damn, I have to stop, the suit choking me to death. Lesson learned; I will have to always wear my leather vest over my suit, the end.

I stop quickly on the side of an off ramp but there is no shoulder. I find a side road to the side road and a parking lot of sorts; I pull into it. Damn this rain is costing me time and the sky is still grey. Throwing my vest on over my suit and putting in my ear buds, I crank the music and GO! The mist on the road is heavy but I make out the road as needed to move forward at a good and solo pace without having to follow a big rig. I am sure I will be hitting rain again but after an hour, it does not come. I have to admit at this time I am just exhausted, cold and wet from fighting the rain as I did. After another hour or two I see a rest stop coming up and decide it is nap time. It may be the middle of the day and the weather may be drivable, but I need to rest, if only for a few minutes.

Pulling into the stop, I see a populated area near the restroom and a very un-populated area near the entrance. I park in the un-populated area, next to a great stretch of well-maintained grass at a nice three or four percent grade. Shut the engine off, dismount, lay down on the graded grass and pass out. I dream of nothing and feel the cool air kiss my face. I can smell something and assume I must be near the sewer ditch, but I just don't care at this point. I lay there, enjoying it all and resting. Eventually the rain starts to kiss my face a little more than it gets real heavy. Then I feel a lot of wet on my face and hear people yelling. Opening my eyes, I find a small dog licking my face and sit up to pet him. Of course, he just barks at me and runs back to his owners. I have only been out for about half an hour I guess and look around, in a complete and lost daze. Darn dog must of pooped near me. I look around and find dog poop, wait; there is a lot of dog poop, everywhere. Yeah, I am laying in the shit.

Every few feet it seems there is more dog poop around me, shaking my head in my helmet and wonder if I am dreaming again. The trees and green in this part of the country are so pretty and so different to what is in my dry western desert. I start to wonder if the effects of being in a different land is playing tricks on my mind. "Wake up Bob, Wake up!" I stand up and lean on a small four-foot-high metal fence post a few feet from me. There is a sign on the post that reads "Dog Area" and shows a picture of a dog, pooping. Somehow, I had chosen to not see the signage and take a nap amongst the dog shit at this rest area. Now I understand why this side of the rest area was vacant. Another car pulls up to this dog area as far away from me as possible and lets another dog out. Wow; what an idiot I must look like in all my gear, leaning on a sign, next to my skoot, amongst the dog shit. I stretch, bend and sip my coffee next to my skoot for a minute then, will my body to walk 100 feet or so to the restroom but first, off comes my helmet as to not scare anybody here into thinking they are under alien attack.

Stepping out of the restroom, a man on an older Harley has pulled up and waves to me. We exchanged hellos and he tells me he is local but going all the way to North Carolina for the cool Smoke Out Motorcycle Rally and hopes to get all the way over there in a few days, he asks me if I have heard of it.

"Oh yeah" I respond. Then the oddest thing seems to transpire on his face, he looks down the front of my vest and reads the red patch on my chest: STAMPEDE. His eyes get as big as dinner plates as he looks at me and asks in a high voice; "Are you one of the racers?"

"Yup," I reply.

Let me forward this conversation by saying very few people know about the Stampede race. When someone notices my patch, I always ask them for an autograph for being cool enough to even know what this race is. It has only happened 10's of times so it's pretty rare. His mouth and mind start moving at a mile a minute with questions like, when did we all leave to start the race and wasn't it started in Barstow California this year?

His eyes get as big as serving plates now as he yells "IT'S MONDAY!"

"Yes," I retort.

"Well I'm a truck driver and I know Barstow California is like 2000 miles that a way!" As he fingers to the west.

"Yes, that sounds about right," I say. Then the awkward silence.

I nod and motion stating I need to get back at it and start walking across the parking lot. He follows me as we chat only, he is following a little too close and as I continue to stretch and move my torso left to right. I actually end up hitting him with my elbows a time or two. This does not seem to faze him as we give our apologies, he goes on and on asking questions in his excitement for this race. Then we get to my cop skoot and his questions go on and on. I start to feel a little impatient at this point but take it all as a compliment and do my best to answer all his questions. I get ready to move again, asking him his name and asking him to look me up at the finish line. It would be good to chat with him there. He shakes my hand and waves as I start the skoot and pull away.

Sometimes I wish one of the Jack Brothers were around to run interference for me on such a talkative person. Jer and Willie Jack are some serious chop builders hailing from Durango Colorado and competitors in this race. They won't get 1st place but they will finish in good standings and against all odds. We like to say there are those who can and then there is Jer who will just do, rather he can or not. His brother Willie is very similar. Both of them can really talk up a storm with anybody, I mean talk faster and with more excitement than most. A few times I have used this to my advantage and taken off while they are running interference with some stranger just talking us up. As soon as I pull away, the Jacks', in haste, can't be out done by me - the one they call 'Slow Bob' - so they mount and take off not far behind me, pass me and I catch me at the next stop, usually chatting it up with some stranger. Personally, I tend to be a little more introverted with strangers than I could be. In the future, I need to be more like the Jacks', just chat it up with whoever and enjoy life a little more.

Refreshed, moving again and excited that someone else is excited about what I - what my competitors and I are all doing out here. I have learned the hard way that when it comes to other riders on the open road, it's easier just to tell them I am in a hurry trying to get to my ailing grandmother's house in the next big town. If I go into too much detail, they tend to get really uncomfortable around me as in a (that's not real or, this jackass is pulling our leg) kind of manner. I'm glad I could be open and honest with this guy and he got it.

My mind wanders back to this race several years ago where my competitor Velarde Gonzalez and I were hopping over each other down the road for several hundred miles of Eastern Arizona, New Mexico and West Texas. From gas station to gas station I would stop and hear him buzz by then I would buzz by and could see him at the station frantically moving to catch up with me and so on. At one stop the store clerk, an older sloppy acting gentleman was a real jerk and had asked me where I was riding too. Thinking he was a rider himself, I told him of this cross-country friendly race we were doing. He laughed and went into a big speech of how stupid us motorcycle riders are. Okay I thought, not a fan, whatever. So, I laughed back at him for jockeying a cash register at his age. His laughter stopped - I got back to the road.

At the next stop the young kid behind the counter came running out when I pulled up and I thought; GREAT: here we go again. Instead he marveled over my beat-up old cop bike and then saw the sticker. For this race we all get to place a sticker on our skoots that's maybe 2.5 by 10 centimeters and they change every year in decoration. It's always an honor to have one of these stickers or in my case; more than one. When this kid saw the sticker he marveled and awed asking me if I was competing in the Stampede?

"Aw, Yes," I answered, ready for anything.

He ran into the small general store in front of me as I hobbled behind him. Grabbed his backpack; he poured the contents out on the counter which included several knives, a few condoms, some hard candy, a hand gun and a few magazines. There was the latest copy of the chopper rag that covers this race. He quickly grabbed a sharpie and asked me for my autograph. I smiled and asked for his autograph in return. Like I said; anyone cool enough to spot me and know what myself and my competitors are doing, is a rock star in my book. I could barely write with the shaking of my hands had endured for that day, but I wrote something on the cover and signed it for him in my common 'Bob, Flying M' signature. I left that stop feeling the same rejuvenated feeling I feel now. Don't need thousands of fans who like this race or follow what we do - hell I don't need any fans. Regular good ole' fashioned hospitality from the road and the fellow movers and shakers running on it is good enough.

But every so often, it's okay to take a shot to the good ego when a stranger in the middle of nowhere asks for your autograph. It reminds me that I; at this moment, am doing something that other people think is cool, maybe even it's something a few others or thousands of others aspire to do. But now, it's me, I am doing it, not them. Bask in it without too much pride, remember where I come from and keep on keeping on, this is after all, a race.

Turnpike Troubadours, "Good Lord Lorrie" *Goodbye Normal Streets,* Bossier City Records, 2012

And just like that, in the mountains now and climbing in altitude as I feel the skoot performing very well. I start doing some simple math in my head and realize, I think it's been a while since my last stop for fuel. I wait patiently but none of those needed gas stations pop up in-front of me and might not as I am on some type of mountain range. The skoot coughs a little losing power as I hastily find the fuel lever inside my left knee, switching to reserve. Running with the road as it goes up hill and down, to the left and to the right. The next listed town on the marquee is 42 miles ahead. Damn, I might be in trouble. I see another exit that seems baron but see a sign for fuel; I take it. Hitting the part dirt, part paved road. Eventually I find the station back in the woods, this must be some type of old mining town. What I would not give for set of shocks right about now.

I walk in and the young lady working the counter gulps at me. I am sure my get up just look ridiculous compared to what she usually sees in her customer based. I pay cash and grab a fruit juice and a sugary treat. Pump fuel then look at my phone and realize my mistress has called me and left a voicemail. I call her back and get her at work. She answers the phone terribly excited to have reached me. I give her the updates and she goes on excitedly about how proud she is of me. She reminds me to be safe and go fast. I thank her and say goodbye in my shaking and tired voice and got to hang up. Getting back down the broken road to the interstate.

I move along thanking God for a woman like her in my life who is happy to just be kind to me and be my friend. We may not be sexual these days, but she still gives me the respect of the man she sees in me. I have to stop my brain; this is all ridiculous. Why would I even talk to her now? When this woman and I started our friendly sexual relationship, I was single as she was but that was months ago. Since then she has chosen another, she has chosen a life that looks good on paper with another man. She has chosen a life that any woman would be proud of and I; her instrument of sexual exploration was left in the dust. The problem is I really had it in my head that she liked me, that she wanted me and had absolute desire for me and her together. That turned out to not be the case. No matter how much I did for her sexually, she was okay to use me and now I have to be okay with that. Together we simply used each other as people do. I served her with every open hand slap, every bite to her soft skin, and inch of pain I gave her. In return, she obediently took all she wanted and thanked me profusely, again and again. Everything has a beginning and an end; this is the end of her and I. No better and no worse for either of us, just: the end. No longer can I think inappropriate thoughts of her, against my new girlfriend, against her new significant other, it isn't fair for either of us. This, yeah this, needs to be a memory. Just a good ole' glad I was there and thanks for the time, memory. I just deserve better and deserve to be good to myself about all of this situation I let myself and my feelings get mixed up in. Maybe I'll still talk to her, we share several friends and there is no reason for me to be rude about it. Just a memory it shall be, and one I will have to thank her for; someday.

Bob Marshall

As I ride out of this little patch of mountains, I hit another storm, this time, without my jacket or suit as I removed it at the last stop. I can see this storm the beginning and the end here at the summit. I will ride through it; taking all the small pains of the rain. I am thankful for all of it as it reminds me that I am alive and with all that I have dished out in my life, even to the back and front side of what's her name I just mentioned; I deserve this. I deserve all of this from the universe; and what a blessing it is to be alive and feel a little pain.

#14

I hope when I grow up, I do not put too much efforts and energies concentrating on the memories of the good ole' days. Wait; is this, MY good ole' days? This, the now is above awesome but in the future, I need to remember to wake up every day and remind myself: today is the day, known as the first day of the rest of your life. Yesterday was awesome but today is going to be better as you Sir, will thrive to fulfill the promise of always doing your best, and letting your best be good enough for today... I am far from my good ole' days, I promise!

My road here is starting to do some... things. The bike is starting to bounce and knock at my teeth, like there are hidden speed bumps grooved into this road. The universe will never throw anything at me that I am not meant to handle, good or bad. Every situation, every life test is, set forth for me I believe to better myself as a thriving member of this human race. All that can ever be done is my very best and my best will be good enough. All I really have to do is learn from each and every experience, bettering myself a little more. Yes, this is work - a lot of work, and it takes a ton of tools that I as a human may not of been born with. It is this, original instinct to move forward and keep moving forward that made me; made all of us, the human race we are known as today.

Personally, I am enjoying the now; greatly. My tired and sore body has slowly given up fighting back at me and is starting to accept its place in the universe. It's not a preferred place, naturally my body prefers to just sit, relax, and light a smoke in a comfortable bed or chair. Yeah sorry o' body o' temple o' mine, none of that soft shit is in the cards today. Be a good sport, be my bitch and shut the fuck up for now. Slowly the road gets better or I am just getting used to it.

Old Crow Medicine Show, "I Hear Them All" *Big Iron World,* Nettwerk, 2006

My head starts to remember for me, I am going to see the arch. The St. Louis Arch has got to be right in front of me just several miles. I don't remember being on this road before so, a real treat for a western born and raised boy like me then; rain. I watch as the sky opens up and starts to drizzle on me again. What is this, the 5th or 6th time today I have been rained on? Well we all know what time it is kids; it's 'suit dance' time. The wet of the rain is fine, after all my mother did make me waterproof for sure, but it's the uncertainty of the road that always makes me nervous. The road gets a little finicky and dicey when mother nature opens up and throws a bunch of water on it. As I put my suit on again, I notice that my back tire is starting to show yellow through the cords as the rubber has really worn away so that will be on my mind as well. I have to wonder how perverted it looks when I bend over and stare up the ass of my skoot, on the side of the road, or at this convenient store, while dancing with my suit. The temperature is not too cold so I should be okay when I do get wet but, I just can't see the end of this storm and it seems to just stretch out for miles across this green and well-watered land full of lush grass and forest. I am going to just accept that everything is going to be wet, and really wet from the look and feel of it. Damn my body is really fighting me and getting into the suit sure is taking longer than it usually does. Slowly but surely, "Go Bob, GO!"

While stopped, I might as well open my bag-o-tricks here on the side of the skoot and throw some extra lube on my chain. I am under a portico of sorts, and I am sure that usually the customers park bicycles here, not skoots but, maybe no one will notice. This does not actually coat the chain as well as the lazy circle ride done in the parking lot but, it sure makes me feel better to have extra grease on this poor metal working hard for me on this rainy day. It's been throwing off a little grease and wax on the sidewall of the rear tire, rear fender, the frame and of course, my baggage. With this skoot leaking a little oil, everything is getting a good dirty coat, let's call it a 'natural occurring water repellent' for now. Also, I notice my 2 taillights have blown out again. Being in the rain without lights on my ass would really suck. I change those out right quick and even add some lens tape as my previous tape job has worn off in the oil, rain and wind of the last thousand miles. I go inside this C store, pee, fill my coffee and grab a few snacks. It's time to move and move well, into the wet and rain I go; again.

The Interstate is there, just inches beneath my feet but damn I can't see that bitch to save my life. The road always has a great way of putting off one hell of a mist in this kind of constant downpour. I just get to sit up and hope to see above it. Behind a big rig to follow them and their big lights in front of me. This keeps me moving slowly but moving then, thunk. And again thunk - thunk.

Damn, this road has some type of crosscut messed up road groove. Slowly but surely the road, about every second in time is beating on me and my machine. I try maneuvering and changing lane positions but nothing; thunk, and thunk, and thunk. Every thunk, the skoot jumps just a little and delivers a mild punch to my kidneys. This has got to clear up soon, it just has to be a bad patch of road that was laid or repaired wrong. Sometimes the road and me just don't agree but it rarely lasts longer than a few miles. For now, stuck in this arse hole of a thunk, doing my best to reposition my body to take less.

I look up ahead as the sun is breaking through and there, on top of the clouds, stands the top of the arch. Just a little top piece of it as it gleams at me. How beautiful it shines as I am amazed in just a day and a half my machine and I have made it so far, from the west, to the gateway of the west. I glance up to it several times while doing my best to deal with the thunks and then, it is gone. I watch as the sky close and darken, feeling it now more than ever. This storm is about to kick my arse. I take a quick picture of my surroundings with a little bit of myself in my suit thrown in and post it. This should let everyone know I am going to be busy for a few hours. I stow my phone in my tank bag which is a little harder than usual given the current state of thunk. Every hit this road is delivering is really beating on both of us; maybe, the machine more than myself. Well you have gotten this far Baby, I mean; Machine, don't fail me now!

Damn, this is starting to be a little ridiculous and borderline crazy, even by my standards. In my head I start to wonder just what in God's name am I doing here? Here in a rainstorm, with wind and wet water and body beating thunks. STUPID THUNKS!!! I am riding an old, self-rebuilt machine with a balding rear tire and the worst part is, I can't eat the snacks I just bought because why? It is wet, like everywhere, and my current state of 'thunk' makes it impossible to eat without biting my damn tongue off. Did I mention I have not gotten much sleep lately? What EXACTLY, am I doing here? I should be home, playing my mandolin or playing with my girlfriend.

Dear God, grant me the serenity to accept the things I cannot change, the courage to change the things I can and the wisdom to know the difference. -Reinhold Niebuhr-

I can't think of anything else to do but pray right about now, pray and breathe. There is just so much to process in my head and my head, is tired, working slower than usual. I have got to remind myself that I do have choices. I have the choice to stop, pull over and find shelter but, what would that do? What am I going to do like hang out in a gas station for hours waiting for this storm to pass? Yeah no, that idea is not going to work. That would just drive me crazy and anxiety to a new level. I find myself changing lanes and moving in weird and different ways in my lane positioning in hopes of getting out of this thunk but no luck. We are just taking the beating of our lives and I do not, know, what to do. As I think this to myself, I have to remember something, something my Pops and so many others remind me of the simple phrase: If you don't know what to do, don't do anything at all. Well, right now I don't know what to do so, that's what I am going to do; nothing. I am just going to sit here, astride my skoot, in the wet, cruising in 4th gear on this balding tire, with my newly aching stomach and just go. This is my condition, my reality, my, now. Yeah, yeah this is going to be as I let it be. If I freak out and let it, this situation will stop me. I have to face a simple fact about me, the only thing that makes me more anxious than running in this weather is stopping.

How badly do I want to keep moving forward? How badly do I really want to be in this race? I need to answer these questions and I need to answer them fast. The answer is I am good for now, just riding, but I am going to take a mental minute and go through the checklist and figure out the math. Staying where I am at the pace of current movement the numbers will show this race could be conquered in just over 2 days with no mechanical issues but, as the road and weather get worse, this could really wear me out and cause me to have to stop to sleep. However, If I stop now, I can rest through this bad weather but, it will put me behind for sure. Seems like the sane choice is clear but this; is cross country chopper racing and there is nothing sane about it.

The biggest problem with stopping is I know I won't rest. I will pace and my mind will wander, leaving me frustrated and even more worn out. No this, this is the way it has to be. I have to go forward no matter how uncomfortable. This pounding, wet and wild weather is my new comfort, my new reality. I have learned the hard way that this is only temporary, only for a short time and not forever. I have an infinite amount of tunability so tuning myself, I will, as I ride out this storm here on my chosen road.

Damn road is wet and slippery, throwing me a little off every so often. A little hydroplaning is good for the soul, reminding me I was right in my chosen extra length in the frame on the design and rebuild of this machine. It is running wonderfully on this road, no matter how much steam screams off these hot exhaust pipes. My welds are really being put to the test now but damn I know they will hold. I suspect they will as they have for the last several years and 10s of thousands of miles already but damn; I hate how much this road is beating on my machine. "Come on and take it ye ole' cop chop, I'm sure the streets of San Francisco were more punishing then this back in the day!"

The wind does it's best to throw me a few feet to the left and right. I have to lay low in my saddle with my head hung down and forward, pushing through it all. Riding it out with my legs nimble, ready to respond to the rage of this weather. Luckily at the last stop, I remembered to put my nitrile gloves on under my leather gloves. I don't remember if it was to keep my hands dry or to keep the gloves from staining them yellow but, right now in all of this at least my hands are dry. My suit is doing an excellent job at keeping me mostly dry as it seems I missed something with fastening the chest correctly and a little cold water is seeping in around my belly button, slowly into my crotch but at this point, I'll take it. My feet are dry as I wrapped them earlier today with plastic bags between my sock and boot. The wind and rain are just kind of falling off of me. I can't eat anything, I can't smoke either, and when I take a swig of coffee it is mostly rain water that collects on top of my tumblers lid - tasting like road.

Mandolin Orange, "Boots of Spanish Leather" (Bob Dylan, *The Times They Are a-Changin'*, Columbia Records, 1964.) *Live on Audiotree* Audiotree, 2014.

The road - this road; what a wet and miserable place but here I am, running on it - astride my righteous machine, and the music plays loud in my ears. I know I'm looking like a fool as all the faces in the little boxes around me strain to see what the crazy man on the funny looking cop bike is doing in this weather; and where the hell is his Mother? "I'm just out here riding and running you boring bitches in your tin cans - the only way I know how!" Oh and, "My mother is at home I am sure; smoking menthols and pounding instant coffee, waiting for my social media posts."

#15

Mumford and Sons, "Timshel" *Sigh No More*. Gentlemen of the Road, 2009

To quote my ole' high school friend, and Rock Star, Tye Zamora, "Anyone who thinks there is no good 'new music' has not heard Mumford and Sons."

On interstate 64 now and the beautiful state of Indiana. The rain has finally stopped so I stop for fuel and a little rest from this storm - needed time to ring the rain out of my gloves. Filling my gas tank then my tumbler with much needed hot coffee. I then push my bike to the side of the gas station in a parking stall and enjoy looking west. I seem to be at the top of some outlook and can barely see over the trees to catch the beams of sunset - if only for a moment but there it is. It feels like I am on top of the world with this big, wet 'after the rain' view. I am more than halfway done with this race, this road, just enjoying the moment; if only for only a moment. Yeah this is something I need to do more often, just stop and enjoy. I am always so busy like most Americans in these United States - I just forget to fucking stop sometimes. Here I am, in a race and just taking in this view I happened to stumble upon while enjoying some hot coffee and a smoke. Lucky me.

My body is pretty dry, and all of its extremities exempt my crotch but I am sure it will dry out eventually out here in the wind. I just have that funk of wet, humid 'not showered in a few days' feeling. I leave my suit on and open it up a little to assist all of me in drying out. With no one seeming to be watching me, I open my front bag, grab my dopp kit and throw some baby powder down the front of my shorts. Aww; fresh as a daisy. Damn my body hurts but soon, soon it will all be worth it. Re-securing everything and getting ready to ride I really feel the drag now. A little stretching while checking my oil and adding some, also adding more lube to my chain. As I inspect it all a bit, I notice something is just - off. I am totally clean. Everything is soaking wet but totally clean: that's weird. Time to move again. Go Bob, GO!

The trees of the land create an almost wall of seclusion from the land itself. I can see the trees, tall, green, and somewhere in all of that is my future road. I quickly check my phone and see that Ella has texted me. I try to call her as my hands will no-longer allow me to text but get no answer, I leave her a message. Excited, ready to move forward through this great night to the best of my abilities.

I'm usually not one to over embrace technology but I have to agree with Robert Pirsig, Author of 'Zen, and the Art of Motorcycle Maintenance' when he wrote, "If you run from technology, it will chase you". So, a few days before this race I learned how to purchase and download a movie on my phone. A light bulb goes off in my head: I find my downloads and start the movie.

He who works with his hands is a laborer.

He who works with his hands and his head is a craftsman.

He who works with his hands, his head and his heart, is an artist.

-- Saint Francis of Assisi

The Movie: 'Greasy Hands Preacher' is on my phone screen and cranking in my ears. Hitting the on ramp and the highway I realize I won't be looking at the screen, and it's a little bright and distracting even at the darkest screen setting but, right now the distraction will keep me sharp on this dark night road. I suspect the road and dark is a simple combination in my head of being a little uncomfortable. I have never been on this road before or in this exact part of the country. It's also a little humid so the air feels different then my home in the desert. This is where I, and other competitors, will start to lose it. I have learned to push through this uncomfortable feeling with the simple idea that other human beings live here, exist here, and travel here so why not me?

After a while, the movie proves to be a great comfort as the land is starting to take its toll. I had gotten to see this movie a few times before this and my friend Shinya Kimura is in it. The movie follows several fellow wrenchers and racers in the motorcycle world. My fellow land speed racer Shinya is one of the main characters. He is out land speed racing on the Bonneville salt flats, sitting in the back of his chase van going into great conversation about his influences in the world of art and all that he builds and creates. He does not speak English in the movie as he is Japanese born and raised. Yes - he does speak English regularly but, prefers to speak Japanese when he has a lot to say or good points to make. He doesn't always have a lot to say but when he talks, I listen; with great interest. His voice, even in Japanese, keeps me comforted and calm as if he was sitting right in front of me and we are having one of our conversations about skoots. Usually his better half Ayu is close by, just in case we have something really important to translate. As most people, I first learned of him and his work through the magazines, then I saw him on a Discovery channel build off and that was it, I was hooked. This man has style and knows how to make a righteous skoot that can ooze mechanical art and haul ass in perfect harmony. Yes, I am a big fan of his. Shinya has been in the motorcycle world for a long time, as a racer and builder, starting in Japan then moving to the states about 10 years ago to the town of Azusa California. My son and crew chief even had his birthday party at Shinya's shop; Chabott Engineering a while ago and let me tell you, the kid scored on the Shinya Swag, I was a bit jealous. And in case you were wondering, Chabott is Japanese for 'Fighting Rooster' I have been told.

Damn it's dark out here. Damn this road feels like uphill. A constant uphill that is terrible steady in the scariest of ways. I pass a big rig every now and then but for the most part, it's just me. I see ahead an alien spaceship lighting up and lowering itself on the road right in front of me. I scream in my helmet and slam the brakes, slowing and ready to fight. These alien fuckers aren't going to take me without a fight, I have seen the movies and know how this works. If I stay on my skoot it should protect me from their alien death rays, or material tracker beams. They probably want me to have sex with all the alien females on their ship. Yeah fuck that, I got my own hotties to deal with and enjoy right here on planet earth. Luckily, I have my suit on for extra protection and I am sure I have a knife or 3, and maybe even a large hatchet or chainsaw in reaching distance. I am sooooo-going to fight right now - totally ready. I got a fucking race to run and NOT IN THE FUCKING MOOD!!! Without warning the overpass passes over my head and I am back under the night sky, with the walls of trees around me, moving down the road, slowly. Well, crap; that was a big waste of mind power and anxiety on my part. The alien spaceship turned out to be a large concrete overpass. Why don't they put reflectors or signage on those things out here? Damn that really scared me and I'm not afraid to state that. I mean could you imagine having to fuck to all the alien women on a big arse spaceship?

Time to speed back up and get moving proper again for the business at hand. I find a big rig in a few miles and hang out a quarter of a mile or so behind, just till I can get my bearings straight again. Also, if there are deer out here as the road signage claims, the big rig should light them up first for me. A quarter mile behind seems right for this, I can relax a little. The alien encounter has passed and I am okay, still moving forward on the road, I think. Unless; this is part of their mind screw and I am really up in their spaceship in a trance and my sexy dad bod is being abused by sexy alien women right about now? Best keep moving forward, push that out of my mind and just move, uphill.

This, feeling; this uphill thing is starting to bug the crap out of me. I adjust my speed a little but can't seem to get the bike to perform any better on this grade. I am beginning to think it's not the road, but my skoot. I keep looking to the side of me, looking for an angle in the trees to see what grade this road is on but it seems the trees are standing perfectly perpendicular to the road which means, this road is pretty flat. I shift down, then shift up. I throttle down to feel any unusual or extra drag on the skoot but nothing, it all feels fine. I need to pull over, somewhere were the big rigs can see me for a mile or two and not run my arse over. Here is a spot, this should work.

I turn on the flashing red cop lights and get my mini mag flashlight out. I spit on the brake calipers and there is no sizzle so: no dragging brake pads. I push the machine for a minute in neutral and all seems fine. I look at my chain which seems at a good tension but, I cannot tell if it's straight or not so maybe it's that? I had just fabricated and welded up a custom chain guard (1.25-inch angle, .187 thick, custom spray painted black) to my frame. It's hardy and will keep a passenger (my hot new girlfriend Ella) from hitting their foot on the chain should it slip off the passenger pegs or guard racks or coffee cup holder or whatever she wants to put her feet on back there. I made sure there were options. Yeah, the new chain guard is sweet and simple, but it does not allow me to see down the chain like I used too. Luckily, I just happened to bring along my chain alignment tool. It's nothing more than a small clamp that clamps to my rear sprocket and it has a thin straight rod perpendicular to that about 6 inches or, I mean, 15 or 16 centimeters, long. I clamp it up and sight down it, keeping it level with the chain while crouched next to the left side of the skoot in a strange fashion and sure as shit, my chain is out of alignment. The big rigs wiz by as I double and triple check; yeah all that beating the road just gave my skoot and I - must have caused something to whack out of place.

Quickly my flashlight goes in my mouth while I grab the few wrenches needed to make short work out of getting this chain to travel on a little straighter path. I wrapped the handle of my mini mag with; you guessed it, hockey stick tape - so I can bite on it a little and, yes, it tastes like used motor oil and cable lube with a hint of road dirt. I loosen the axle with a big arse crescent wrench and the axle stays with a 12mm and smaller crescent wrench as needed. This loosens everything up a little for me, so I kick the back tire to the left and right as needed with my arse on the ground. Usually I could do this with some arm power when the machine is up on a bench in front of me, but I seem to be shy of said bench here on the side of this interstate so - kicking it is. With everything a little tight, I start the skoot, engage the clutch and move forward a few feet, then let it roll back. I do this all in an effort to work out any kinks or hidden issues with the 'very fucking important' relationship between the sprockets and chain. A little more checking and tuning and bam; it looks straight, to the best of my ability. While I am crawling around on this asphalt in the middle of nowhere with the big rigs flying by; might as well double check all my welds on the frame, and anything else I can think of - all looks good. I designed and rebuilt this rear end myself, so I know it; intimately. I see nothing odd or out of place, it all looks good and true. Everything gets tightened as needed and the tools get store back in the saddle bag. I pat the side of my tank in a loving fashion and admiration of all this machine is putting up with. My hands get wiped off - helmet and gloves go back on. "Go Bob, GO!"

Running again, the skoot does feel better but that might be in my head. It is always when we do a little work on something our minds want to tell us we have fixed it; a placebo effect. I have got to give this one some time to see if it had any real effect on my power but - here we are, my skoot and I - getting down the road and passing again the same big rigs we passed a while ago; who just passed us a few minutes ago. I can only imagine what those guys are thinking and who is this 'WE' bit I am referring too? Does my machine and I count as a 'WE'? Damn, I must be getting tired, I mean it's only a machine 'we' are talking about; right?

The movie was playing for those several minutes on the side of the road and is now over, I turn my phone's screen off. I have to think for a minute and make sure I am comfortable with this rear end business. The skoot is righteously pulling well now but it still feels; off - I think. Maybe it's just something to do with the equilibrium in the depths of my brain. That feeling like I am moving uphill is very real even though everything else tells me I am on a flat road. I need to accept this as the truth, for now. Soon; I am sure I will start to suffer from moving sickness. The sickness just means I will get nauseous when not moving, all the more reason to keep moving. Also, I am starting to hear and feel my left ear problem. After riding for a day or two, my left ear starts to ring with all the noise of the wind against my helmet. I have been told my eardrum in that ear shifted some time ago and it is currently reminding me of this.

Eventually I find another gas station, going through the motions, with tired and calm ease. I check the chain alignment and tension again and everything looks good as I smile at my success. I purchase extra beef jerky, some more hard candy and even some of those small yummy donuts to go with my coffee. DAMN YOU LITTLE YUMMY DONUTS FOR BEING SO FUCKING YUMMY!

I rub my ears for a minute and try to massage the whistle and hum out a bit but to no avail. I know this extra noise will bug the crap out of me and keep me awake - pissed off and moving forward. I will just accept it as my new norm for now. Damn, I am slowing down; I mean I can really feel just how slow all my motions are. Yesterday I did almost 1500 miles, today I might do 1000, tomorrow or in a few hours I will need to do another 500 to get this cross-county chopper racing business taken care of. Only time will tell how it will all work out. For now, my plan is just to keep moving forward.

Mumford and Sons "I Will Wait" *Babel,* Universal Island Records, 2012

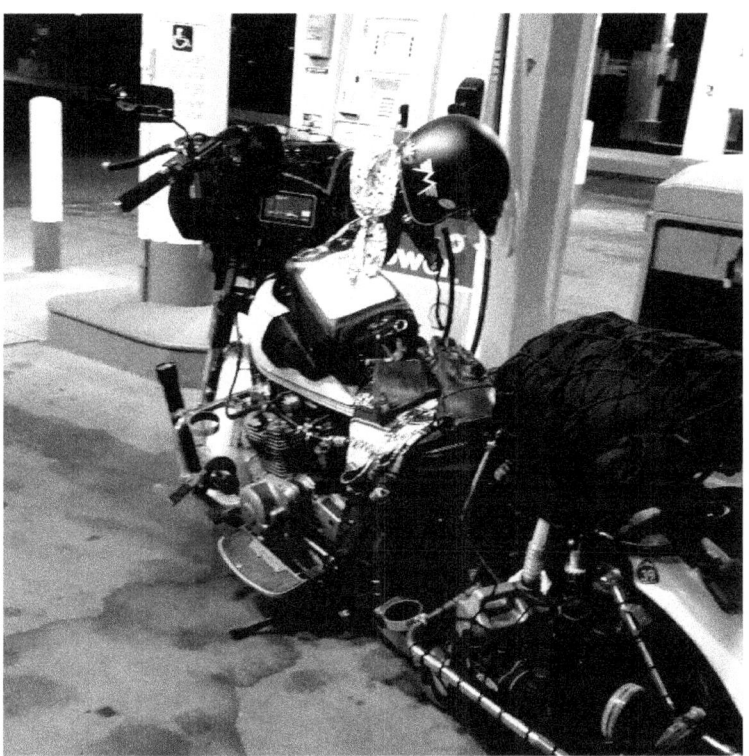

Back on the road - as dark as dark can be. The weather is going well, the road is going well, the skoot is going well, a little off but still moving so I will run with it and be comfortable with it. I, on the other hand, not so much. I start going through the motions, slapping myself a little, opening and closing my face shield, spitting water back in my face only to spot up my face shield. Eating and chewing lots of hard candy even though it seems I already had some. I had apparently forgotten about this at the last stop and purchased some more. Now I have pockets and bags full of hard candy. I find my sunflower seeds after a while and start chewing and spitting, leaving behind sunflower seeds and their remains all over the inside of my face shield. Wow, what a mess but I just don't care right about now. The stink I am starting to take on inside my helmet is much more distracting. I have experienced this before; the smell of my hair and head wrap and helmet liner all mixed together in a great big uncontrollable 'manly' stink. I remember changing my head wrap earlier in the day but at this point, it seems I get to live with my smell. The smell of my greasy dirty hair mixed with the road all held under my face shield and filling my nostrils. The problem is it comes and goes, with the wind. A little side breeze or turning of my head and bam, there it is. If I can face forward the whole time I do not smell it as much but I do turn my head sometimes or pass a big rig and there it is - enough to annoy the shit out of me for forever and a day. I need to put my small beanie on next time I stop, IF I can remember to do that. Maybe leave my wrap tied to the bars for a few hours to dry off and flap some of the stink off in the wind.

Eventually there comes a point, that point where things are just not making sense. The aliens are still around, but now they are in the reflectors on the road. Just standing there; waiting for me to make a mistake so they can take me. They also brought their friends: the dinosaurs. They are reaching out for me through the trees. The road, this road, this damn road is beating me every so often like a dominatrix that won't let up no matter how many safe words I throw at her. I am not into that kind of sexual play and it is starting to aggravate me to no end. I finally seem to have lost it and start looking down; yelling at the road. "Listen; you are mine. You are my road, for me to run and race on as I see fit. I pay my taxes for your creation, construction and maintenance. YOU WILL NOT CONTROL ME! I AM THE NAVIGATOR! I WILL BE CONTROLLING YOU! YOU WILL STOP BEATING ON ME!!!"

Damn, I need to stop. I hold still at this moment in time almost frozen on my skoot, embarrassed as I realize my insanity.

I know at this moment; my anxiety is getting the best of me. I breathe - the one action that can concentrate me on the now, keeping me absolutely in the moment, this moment, the here and now of 75 mph in the dark. "Just breathe, breathe with all your mind, body and soul Bob" I whisper to myself. Reaching into my left vest pocket, I turn my music off. My reality has shifted from mine to that of something I am not familiar or comfortable with. I have a choice, a decision to make. I can stop and wait but, wait for what? To make it comfortable - maybe wait for daylight? Or I can make it mine, grab it by the arse and make it mine like a mother fucker. The big picture needs to be in my sights, I need to see with clarity who, what, where, why and how - I am. This will take a lot of thinking, and smart thinking at that. I don't know what to do right now so, I will choose to do nothing at all. I will continue on this road, embrace the beatings as a blessing to keep me awake, embrace the pain to remind me I am alive. I am alive and flying fast on this road astride this righteous skoot of mine. I will make my uncomfortable, comfortable for me - as the human race has for many thousands of years. I am a part of this human race, and I will be doing this, here and now, this road, this race, just fucking running.

Ryan Bingham "Hard Times" *Mescalito,* Universal Music Group Nashville, 2007

    I arched my back, move a leg forward, move a leg back, then again – skootin' yoga. I have learned the long and hard way that if I move my body, it will naturally stay awake. As long as I keep moving my body just a little, my mind will focus on that, that movement and keep my eyes open. I put my left leg out, straight out into the wind, slowly feel the resistance and work my aching knee against it. This action takes muscle, slowly pumping my leg out, then back again, 3 times. Now the right leg, slowly pumping straight out; 1, 2, 3. My back now, slowly forward then relaxed; 1, 2, 3. I work through every part of my body that can be worked or stretched in this way, from the bottom to the top then relax back into my riding position.

I pull my water from my front net and take a few swigs - slowly with great intent and re-install the bottle back into the net. I remove my left-hand glove and place it under my right throttle hand to hang on to it. Rummaging through my tank bag now, I can't seem to find my pack of smokes. This happens sometimes but I have a plan. I stop rummaging for a minute then slowly try again. Eventually I find them, on the wrong side of the tank bag. This rummaging through the tank bag always has to be done slowly, minding not to spill anything out onto the road.

I pull a smoke from the pack with my teeth, hold it there while stowing the pack and push the lighter down. I feel for it after a few seconds; not yet. I feel again and it has popped out. It glows like a roman torch in my face. I look into my reflection in the rear-view mirror to line up my smoke with the lighter and inhale. I have to do this as my goggles and face shield will not allow me to glance down enough to see the end of the cigarette. With the last glow from the heat of the lighter, I find its port and re-install it. I breathe in, deep drags of tobacco filling my lungs and soul with this poison that will kill me some day if I let it. Scratch my nose, itch my face, run my fingers around my neck between the suit and me. Just a made-up relaxing moment.

I take the time to slowly check my phone only to realize that I have not heard from Ella in several hours. I have to think for a minute and remember I might be 2 hours ahead of her by now I think and should have heard from her. Well maybe she got busy with something. I turn the phone off and do my best to concentrate on the road. It's so dark out here and I have been out here a while, I may no longer even be in Indiana anymore. I actually start to wonder if I am still on interstate 64. That is where I am supposed to be right? After some time, I notice signage reminding me, I am on interstate 64; that's a good sign - literally.

I see something, something off to my left, a man riding a big black Harley next to me. As I focus more on it, I realize it's my good friend and fellow Abate member: Jack Howell. His grey beard is flapping in the wind as his arms are stretched high to reach his tall ape hanger handlebars. Wait; this doesn't make any sense. Jack would not ride out of Southern California these days let alone all the way out here. After a few seconds I see the back of his Abate vest fade in front of me as he pulls away. He was just an illusion. Jack is one of my dearest friends, several years older than me, he is always eager to assist me or chat with me about this or that. Riding next to him is always fun as he is constantly pushing speed and having a good time going a little faster than we really should. Damn I could use Jack out here right about now.

My music is back on, so I turn it down just a little, so I have to concentrate a little harder to hear it - just another small game I play with myself keep me awake. Feeling my eyes sag again, it is time for some more yoga. Slowly but surely, this time from my head and neck, down to my feet.

As I exercise my right ankle I look over and see something way too close to me. It startles me - almost scares me. My Pops on his big old man Black Honda, just cruising right next to me. A sight I have witnessed many times with all the miles we have conquered together. His eyes are dead ahead forward as he concentrates with intent on the road. I know now - clear as day this is only an illusion. I embrace it and start signaling to him, asking him what the time is while pointing at my wrist. He looks over to me just for a second then looks forward again, with no response. Maybe he is tired of that joke, or maybe, he is leading by example.

Oh, that old joke of mine that makes me laugh every time. He rides, pointing at his watch while we are on the road, after a few comments of such from him on our time and miles; I get annoyed. I just want to enjoy the road, go forward and move well, no reason to worry about exact time while on the road via skoot. At a gas station, I steal his cheap watch he wraps around his handlebars: get a few miles down the road, ask him what time it is and enjoy the look on his face when he sees his cheap watch is not where it is supposed to be. As he looks over at me, I show it to him in my hand, smile and chuck it into the wind. He flips me off as I smile back and twist throttle.

My Pops is so concentrated on the road ahead of us now and not paying me any attention. What kind of dad does that anyways? In almost annoyance; I look over my left shoulder to switch lanes to outrun his ghostly image so close to me. I do this and catch something out of the bottom right of my eye. I miss a dead animal carcass by inches or centimeters that was sitting in the slow lane; right where I was just riding. If I had more energy right now, I might be freaking out about this. I look back to my right and see the ghostly image of my Pops has disappeared back into the dark night while I am still moving forward with my rubber side down - in one piece.

Time to make some decisions for my safety; stop or keep going. Crap, there it is, a blessing I will take; 'Rest Stop Ahead' reads the reflective sign; decision made for me. Pulling off and once again, find a few other competitors resting. Shutting off the skoot, I roll a few spaces away from them, fall off the skoot - grabbing my saddle rag off my seat on the way down. My mind is trying very hard to keep moving but I view it as a movie playing on the boob tube while I separate my mind from my body. "You have to get a few good hours of sleep: this is nonnegotiable Bob Marshall." After a few minutes, I am asleep and totally dead to the world, with no hot threesomes involved.

#16

"Bob is right over there! Hurry up!"

"What?!?"

"Bob is asleep right over there!"

The fuck? Is this some type of dream? Maybe another sex dream? What the fuck is going on? I roll over on the hard pavement of the parking lot with my head hanging out in the driving lane. My eyes show me 50 or so feet up the parking lot in the middle of this dark night; something. Something I can almost make out; my eyes are almost in focus. A skoot or, the back of a skoot with an outline of someone sitting on it, in a strange way, maybe a very tall person? I don't know. I slapped my hand on the pavement in front of me trying to push myself up, trying like hell to make out what I am seeing. I focus hard, and straight. I can see now my fellow competitors and friends Pete and Jen who are racing 2 up after just getting married. It's easy to figure out its them because adorning the back of their skoot, strapped on the upright bag is a large sign stating: "JUST MARRIED". Pete has an awesome self-built custom Yamaha with a very distinct V4 engine. I see Jen pointing back at me while Pete, is dismounting and I assume running into the restroom. The noise must have been Jen yelling my name. Whatever; I roll over and go back to sleep.

3 seconds later I jump up - eyes wide open and run but cannot, my tired and worn body won't have it. Like a cannonball; I put myself to my knees then upright then, trying like hell to walk up the slight incline to the restrooms. Why is it everything seems to be uphill tonight? I stop after a few steps, I need to change my shirt and take a shower in the sink, something to make myself feel human again. I stumble back, open my personal bag mounted on the front of my skoot retrieving a clean long sleeve shirt and my dopp kit just in time to see Pete jumping back on his skoot in a sideways fashion as Jen is still on the back and never dismounted. Off they roar, leaving me holding my bag and feeling low and slow in this dark rest stop. This race is sooooooooo fucking on now if I can only remember how to walk.

This is all my fault. A few states back, maybe 24 hours ago I saw them at a gas station, and we compared notes on how the ride was going for a few minutes. Pete was on fire having the time of his life with his new bride Jen hanging on with her beautiful smile ear to ear. Now I have to tell you; Pete was in the armed services and retired a higher-ranking officer, so he is built like a brick wall. Jen is like 20 years his junior and pretty well built herself, together they can be a little intimidating for the average person. Lucky for me they are my friends and on my side. As the three of us were dancing around our skoots and conversed, another competitor pulls up on an older, 4 speed Harley. He dismounted his younger southern-self and heads straight for the greasy spoon of a restaurant next to the gas station. He stopped to say 'hello' to all of us but goes on about how ready he is for a full stack of flapjacks. As he walked away, the rest of us are all holding our tongues till Jen in her questioning voice asked; "So people can stop and eat on this race?"

Pete and I had a quick glance at each other: "NO" we retort to her; in unison and with gusto. With that, we all mount up. With them as pilot and piloteer astride that beautiful chopped skoot, my final statement was simply: "I don't need to finish first but damn I hope I beat both of you." That was really kind of stupid on my part, like telling someone you are going to 'sue them in court' before you actually do. Now, a day later - Pete and Jen are on a mission, hell bent to kick my arse in this race. Lucky for me my brain recognized the thump whine thump of that beautiful Yami V4 engine. It woke me up and now I need to run now like a mother fucker. "GO BOB, GO!!!!"

Okay, wait, why am I removing items from my bag when I can just take the entire bag? Damn, Bob! I throw the shirt and dopp kit back into the bag feeling like an idiot and grab the entire bag. Stumbling now but upright into the restroom and finding a stall, unsnap the overalls catching them as they hit my knees.

I sit down on a toilet and stretch and bend my body. I reach for my phone only to realize I left it on the skoot; again. I have to sit here for a few minutes and make sure this business is taken care of appropriately. Wipe, wet-one wipe, flush, stand up, walk out of stall tripping on the door as usual with my large frame of a body. Remove shirt; wipe body with old shirt then remember, I have a small towel. Wet it and start wiping, my face, neck, body, armpits and crotch, front, then back. Deodorant, baby powder for the boys in front and some for my back side as well. A little balm on the bum too. I can feel I have what might be referred to as 'bed sores' or 'seat sores' but they are light and manageable as this point, I hope. I mean I can't see back there so; this should work for now. Some sunscreen for the dark morning, new shirt then re-snap overalls. Now the fun part; brushing of the teeth. Nothing seems to trick my mind more than these simple actions that it's time for a new day. Aww, shiny whites and ready to go. Now I have to pee again; weird, must be one of those middle-aged things I hear the older guys talking about. Into the trash my towel goes and everything else back into my bag. I am ready for the new day.

Back to the skoot; my phone is still there. A quick walk around with my flashlight and all looks good and sound except I can see some white showing through on my rear tire. It seems I have worn through the tire a little and it is exposing itself. Well I can't blame it, the poor tire is 2 years old and has been across this country already, on this rigid. Rigid frames give the back tire a lot of extra added stress and after a few thousand miles they let you know about it. Damn this is amateur of me. I could have just replaced it and not had this issue here and now. Stuffing the flashlight in my mouth, I rummage around in the saddle bag and find a tire pressure gauge to check it out. I usually like my tires a little proud, around 38 or 40 pounds per square inch of air pressure or, psi. Just 10 percent or so above the machine's factory recommended air pressure, depending on the skoot. I am a little heavier than the average rider so a little extra air in the rear tire is usually needed and good insurance. Removing the Schrader valve cap; I plug in my tire pressure gauge, it reads at 36 psi but the tire is hot which will cause the pressure to read a little shy of what it actually is so it might be a little less - as much as 10 percent. This means closer to 40 psi: decisions - decisions. If I can keep my speeds down when the road is hot, I should be okay. It's still dark as can be as I light a smoke, re-pack and re-stow all, double check everything, button up my vest; okay now it's: Go Bob, Go!

The trick to all of this is simple management. Most of what I do as a mechanic is just management. The more I can manage before racing across this country the better off I will be. Of course - shit happens - and the better I can manage on the fly or by the seat of my pants, the more I will not die. It took me a long time to learn how to look into the future, too see what I might need in life to repair something or keep something going down the road and make it all work. The easiest way to do something is usually a little over thought and the laziest way to do something. My Pops is the laziest man I know. He can look at something, ponder on it for a few moments and fix it or figure it out for you the easiest, or laziest, way possible to fix it. I suspect my son has some of these traits as well but personally, I tend to just jump into something and see where it takes me. Most of the time it is not the easiest road but damn I have fun. As I get older though I have learned to embrace my pop's laziness and do my best to stop, relax, look into the future and figure it out; the lazy way. Someday I'll be older, wiser, and lazier but for now here I am with a balding tire somewhere on the east side of Indiana or maybe West Kentucky. I am okay with all of that.

I have learned that most people just don't seem to get out and travel like I do. As a boy I was blessed to hang out with my Pops many times in his room while he packed a small suitcase of whites and a garment bag full of nice suits then caught a plane somewhere for business. Every so often, he would just load up the company station wagon with all of us kids and take us with him if he was just hopping somewhere in the southwest. I was blessed by these experiences and above all: how to pack. As I mentioned earlier; packing on a skoot is a little different - packing on an old chopped racing skoot like this with all the tools and extra chemicals is WAY different. There really is no magic to any of it, just good ole' experience with a side of management. I figured out what I needed to do by just doing it;

trial and error, process of elimination. Hell, I have left shit on the side of the road for the next guy because I brought it and did not need it or simply thrown shit away because it broke or is not serving me. If I am just hoping across a few states for a few days; I will just bring a few shirts, my dopp kit, 1 pair of socks and maybe some undies. My foul weather gear takes up most of the room and that, is really what I need; not spare shirts or undies. I make sure what I pack is what I need. I love layers and might even try on my clothing before leaving for said trip just to make sure nothing impedes the movement of my arms or legs. People (mostly younger) have told me they bring extra pants everywhere they go because they are afraid they will shit themselves in the middle of nowhere. They of course have never used them because, who really shits themselves in the middle of nowhere? Pull down your pants and take a crap people, use your extra bandana or whatever to wipe your bum and get back on your skoot. It seems we all just get hung up on the little things and we let those said little things slow us down way too much. Where I am right now, others have been or call it home and they have survived just fine so why not me?

Damn, to imagine a future with all kinds of people, all wonderful Americans riding skoots around this cool continent of ours. All exploring, visiting, vacationing while on 2 wheels, saving fuel and money. All just getting away from the mundane life of everyday and hitting the open road with family and friends or just as solo as can be, oh what a wonderful world that would be. I hope someday as a country we grow up enough to make all these things a reality, but I digress - for now.

#17

Slowly my skoot accelerates with me astride it, hitting the on ramp and back to my old friend; road. I didn't care who I woke up when I fired this machine up. I was only there for an hour or two but here we go. I get through the gears at my leisure, taking my time to feel out the rear tire. It all feels fine, the road is cool so chances of this thing blowing out in the next few hundred miles might be 50/50. I can take those odds so back to our regularly scheduled race pace it is.

Having something like a G.P.S. to fiddle with is always a good idea on a ride such as this. That statement however is superseded by; having something to play with that does not want to play back; is just bad fucking distraction. I started this race with this old model in hopes of it assisting me in finding gas stations and keeping track of time. Of course my Pops noticed it and also noticed that it had the time on it at the start of the race, commented to me about it and yes, it earned him my scowl and middle finger; oh the small things we can do as grown ass children to make our old parents laugh. This G.P.S. kept messing up on me as to where I was located, and the poor screen just could not handle all the banging and vibrations of my chopper and has left the job of sniffing out gas stations to my nose. Sure, this may cost me a stop or three but an efficient gas stop at an efficiently running gas station is better than pre planning a gas stop only to be let down by some fangled new G.P.S. contraption that's fucking up. My Pops did not have G.P.S. back in the 1970s when he was riding his old cop chop around. I guess back then with their little peanut tanks and twin Harley engines they all set out to see these United States of America and visit every damn gas station along the way. Good for those old dudes doing what they did on righteous old skoots slowly but surely.

I want the small overpriced gas stations right next to the road. The big truck stop ones are cool as they most likely carry oil I might need or bulbs or whatever else I could possibly imagine in the middle of the night. But during rush hours and busy day times, the small overpriced stations will be faster and more convenient no matter how bad their coffee may be. I don't mind the few extra dimes in price per gallon of fuel, I mean it's not like I'm fueling my Ford Excursion or anything. I just need 5 or 6 gallons every time I stop, some coffee is nice of course and a restroom but above all; I need a little space from people. Everyone, from old men to young women, likes to stop and chat with me. The attention this skoot and I seem to demand can get a little overwhelming causing personal distraction as I love to hear people and their short, not long, stories of their riding experiences. But sometimes I just have to take care of the business at hand and pass up things I love, like other people and their stories. It is funny to see how much the fuel costs change or go down the more I get to the middle of the country which makes no sense to me, but price is always determined in the marketplace.

On my first stampede I had gotten a nice little G.P.S. that I enjoyed using for its timed read outs. How much I was moving, how much I was stopped, average speed and a few other cool bits of information I enjoyed knowing. When I had gotten to the east coast, it started messing up telling me I needed to plug it into a computer and reset it, pay for more software, blah - blah. I did not have time for that as I was in the middle of a race, in the middle of nowhere. I figured out later you are supposed to re-purchase mapping software for these units and re-register them or something every year or two. Wow what a racket, and no thanks, you corporate asshats. I had to manually reset that unit every hundred miles or so just to get to the finish line. As I did this, being ever so faithful to my G.P.S. it got me lost once or twice but eventually found the finish line. Back then the race ended at a nice golfing resort and hotel. This G.P.S. took me around a side, not the main entrance. I realized that I had passed the front entrance to the hotel or finish line too late and just followed my G.P.S. as I could, make a right then another quick right. Still following my trusty G.P.S. unit, I hit some weird looking driveway where the skoot stopped and I - flew over the handlebars. I had hit some loose white dirt; hands and belly first. Turning back to see my cop skoot propped up on its side and buried almost half a meter in white dirt. I jumped up and realized I was in a small forest of some sort, in the dark. There were road signs amongst the trees as if streets were supposed to be here but there were no streets, just this white soft quicksand type of dirt.

I picked the skoot up, re-bent the handlebars with some muscle then re-started my poor battered machine. I needed to get out of there and get to the finish line. As I engaged the gear and let out the clutch, the bike would not move. It was spraying dirt off the back tire and stuck in the perfect sized hole I had just made; not going anywhere anytime soon. Shutting off the bike and grabbing the flashlight hanging from the handlebars, it was clear I was stuck as stuck could be. The skoot was really wedged in the soft white ground and I, had to dig it out.

Stopping for a moment, I could hear people laughing and talking. The hotel was literally 100 feet in front of me, but the forest of pine trees blocked my view. I considered walking through and asking some fellow Stampeders for assistance but damn, I would never live that down. I put back on my gloves, grabbed a large crescent wrench to use as a shovel and began to dig my skoot out. I had been awake for a day and a half at this point after only sleeping a few hours a night for the last several days. I think the relationship between myself and those G.P.S. units may take a little while before it is all ironed out correctly. Please read: "Fuck those things!" They are unreliable, lose signal and cause accidents. These days I never follow them, I simply carry maps and write with sharpie marker on some masking tape I put somewhere on my tank or tank bag. I stop for a few minutes, check my maps, write down on the tape with a sharpie where I have to go and done; I got directions that don't lose signal or lead me into sand pits.

I reach down to turn on my music only to realize, I forgot to put my earbuds in, they are flapping around my head, hanging on to the bandana around my neck. It is going to be a quiet ride for a while, and I am okay with that for now. Just me, my skoot, my road and the cool dark morning air kissing every inch of me except my butt which is planted on my saddle rag in the seat. This kind of cool quiet is rare in today's society. Oh, sure it gets plenty quiet at nighttime where I live but you still hear the city moving with its electric transformers, lights, trains and automobiles. Out here in the dark country, there is none of that, just wind and road with the occasional big rig and the roar of my awesome engine.

Softly, I can see the sky in front of me begin to lighten up and slowly show me it's colors of oranges, blues, and so many other pretty colors my brain cannot process. It's beautiful, beautiful beyond what most of us ever get to experience, as most would never be here on a skoot so early in the morning. I breathe, I thank God and the universe and all other positive forces around me for all the beauty granted to me at this moment. Damn, I wish I could describe this in words and give it it's true value of beauty, but I cannot.

I swig down the rest of my cool coffee and it occurs to me I really have no idea how far I have come since I last filled up. I try to do the math in time, then in miles... nothing. I suspect I am going to need fuel soon enough but for now, I am just going to enjoy these sights, sounds, smells and energies I have been blessed to witness. Moving along I wait, and wait, and see no real signage stating towns or civilization ahead. Usually this is where I would get a little anxious but this morning, I have no energy for that. The bike stutters a little after a while; I reach down with my left hand and try to find the fuel pet cock but cannot. I have to pick a straight course, hold the sputtering bike steady and look down, see it, put my hand on it and flip the lever 180 degrees to reserve. Most of my machines have the petcock where I can flip it from - on – to - off - to - reserve, but they all seem to be in just a little different place under the left side of the tank.

Well - now I know how much fuel I have. The good thing about these old cop bikes is they have a tall reserve. When serving in the field, a moto cop would simply ride till it hit reserve then get back to the pumps at the station usually on their lunch breaks. I know I can go for 30 or 40 miles maybe on reserve but damn I would hate to push it. I do carry a small metal water bottle of extra fuel; back up to my back up. After several more miles, there it is, with the bright light of the morning shining behind it on the left side of the highway, a petrol station. Exit, cross the highway, turn left into the station only to realize I am on the on ramp of the highway, not the stations driveway. I stop, flip a bitch, go up the wrong way on the on ramp and back to the road, left, then left, then success, I am in the gas station. Luckily there was no traffic around to see me make that maneuver or worse - law enforcement.

As I dismount, I can feel my body revolting, angry at me for all I have put it through. I stop, remove my helmet and start walking. A few laps around the small station and some stretching should keep my body happy for a little while, maybe. It also warms me up, as my body aches and curses me for my lack of a physical training or fitness program. After the walk and stretch I refuel, lube my chain a little and check the oil, yup in need of half a quart, this poor engine is doing it but damn it is losing a little in the process. Grabbing my coffee tumbler, I make my way to the stations small convenient store and enter as the two middle aged and grey-haired women yell, "Morning hon."

"Aww... good morning," I say back as it seems to be a shift change time. I am the only one in the store with them. I fill my coffee, grab a fruit juice, 2 bananas for a dollar and some beef jerky: plain. As one of the women cashiers rings up my purchases I ask, "Do you know how far it is to Richmond?"

"Oh yeah sug, Richmond's place is just right down the road here a piece. Go that way then, make the second left on the dirt road. Just mosey on up to the 3rd gate and honk."

"Aww... no," I explain, "I mean the town of Richmond, to the -- ?"

The second cashier interject to the first, "Yeah, Richmond sure is a nice feller, I can't believe his wife just left him, did you hear about that?"

"Oh, I heard about it, I heard ALL about it if ya know what I mean," and she throws me a wink.

"Yeah, it's so strange she would leave him especially with how he dresses," as they chuckle together.

Oh my God what the hell did I walk into? I pay and as the first cashier is handing me my change she stops, turns around and says to the second cashier; "Wait, how would you know about his ya know what?"

The first cashier retorts with, "Honey, how would you think I know? A woman needs some attention sometimes as well and Richmond is just the man if you know what I mean!"

The second cashier jumps up with mild anger stating; "Wait there just a minute - HUN; I have been sleeping with Richmond!"

The first cashier squares up the second and states, "Ya have? Na-ah, ya haven't! I have been sleeping…"

"HAVE A NICE DAY LADIES" as I run out the door, stow my goods in the tank bag and get the hell out of there before shit gets ugly. It's like 5 in the morning, why are these women just figuring out they have both been sleeping with the same married man and getting mad at each other for it? Jeez ladies; you all have some serious issues to work out and it's not going to be in front of me, too early for that crap!

Back on the road now, away from the commotion of those issues. I still never found out how far Richmond, Virginia is.

Wait, what happened to Louisville? I have to stop all other brain processing and remember going through a larger city last night, that must have been Louisville, maybe I slept in Kentucky last night? Well, I give up on that right now, I just don't care. Onward and forward, I forgot to put my earbuds back in and forgot to take my suit off. Maybe it can wait. I open up the front of it just enough to let a little air in without it strangling me and undo the arm cuffs. After half an hour; it cannot wait. I also forgot to use the restroom at the last stop and for good reason. There was most certainly going to be a fight of sorts between those 2 ladies and I did not want to be around when they start throwing toothless blow job comments at each other or pulling out each other's thinning grey hair.

There is nothing around me, damn. I see a small off ramp to what looks like a farming community; I'll take it. Parking on the shoulder of the off ramp - kind of, I take my suit off. There is a small hill a few feet away, I run down it enough to not be seen by traffic, unzip, flop out and pee. Crap, I hear car tires on the gravel behind me. I hear a whistle and turn my head to see an old sedan of a car full of young female teenagers all waving, laughing and whistling at me peeing on the side of the road. They can't see my junk or anything, but I am pretty sure it's obvious what I am doing. Yup, it can get exciting here in Kentucky pretty early on a Tuesday morning. Oh, how proud my daughter would be of me at this moment, I can hear her now: "Gosh dad, you are soooooo embarrassing."

I zip up and run over to the bike and try to text on my phone a 'good morning' to my daughter but I cannot. I call her instead but no answer. Darn, so I leave a message just telling her good morning and that I am doing fine, and I love her. I secure my suit in its bag while eating a banana, throw on my vest, earbuds, helmet, gloves, turn the key on, tap my start wires together and off I go.

I hit the road thinking of my beautiful daughter and all the life and excitement she has brought me. I know she is a little mad with me lately, but I have to let her just be her. It seems appropriate really for her not to want to hang out with me at this stage in her life - no matter how much I wish she was just happy to be my daughter and let me be her dad. Time is what it is and right now, no matter how much I dislike it, it's just her time to be totally independent, away from her dad.

When I was a young boy, my Pops explained to me that everyone expected more of me as I was the oldest son, the namesake, etc. I remember every time I wanted to complain about something my Pops could always shut me down with simply listening to me then reminding me that I am the oldest son. As I went through life, I always remembered that more was expected from me compared to others as I am expected to be an above average person. Unfortunately, the downside to this attitude in life is I have great expectations of the ones I love and yes - to a fault sometimes. I could never expect more from my daughter academically as she performs in that field far above and beyond my wildest dreams. Sometimes I do worry about her with her attitude on things but that is all part of the magic that makes her; her. As she was my first child, there was a lot of learning I got to do as a parent. She is terribly smart and can figure anything out on her own, but she has to figure it out her way these days. If I assume or put too great of an expectation on her, she will resist and bite back, and rightfully so.

Amanda Palmer, "Ukulele Anthem." *Theatre Is Evil* 8ft. Records, 2012

Blaring in my ear, something about playing a ukulele. I am a mandolin player, as such I do not particularly care for the ukulele let alone it being sang to me too; "play your ukulele." My daughter put this song on my mp3 player as a joke to me a few years ago. I have to laugh at her sense of humor, good for her and lucky me. I listen to the entire damn song enjoying all the memories of how much that little girl, now a young woman, taught me about love and life.

#18

"Young men that roam, take heed to this, the call of the road, it can be so unkind. It will lead you on, like a big ole' kiss, and a wasted life, is all you will ever find".

- Doc Watson, Call of the Road.

How long is this damned road to Richmond Virginia? This interstate 64 seems to go on and on forever. On the map it looks right around the corner and the math is not adding up to my tired worn out brain. I am simply not adding up. Lucky for me right now I am the man of travel with full purpose and true destination although maybe; I would not mind a good, 'wander about' right about now. Just a relaxing excuse to ride from hotel to lunch spot and so on; Ride to Eat - Eat to Ride or, Ride to Sleep - Sleep to Ride. Dammit, how nice sleep sounds. It seems so tangible for me and yet, so far away. I could just pull over, get a room and lay my body down but I promise, my mind would not allow it until I cross the finish line of this damn race. The running of the mind of an anxious human man, the fear of missing this race or placing poorly in it will push me and my performance. I am here to compete in this human race, so compete; I will.

It occurs to me that if I had some fancy G.P.S. system or even one that worked correctly it would probably tell me how far Richmond is from my current location. I know I have my phone and could look it up but, my hands and fingers are just shit right now; I'm barely clutching my bars. I mean I have to take turns on which hand holds the bars at this point, switching between my right and left just to ride. Damn, I love this crude cruise control. Best to just keep running on this road and tune my want for numbers out of my mind. Go Bob, Go! We all know that as American consumers, we are used to things happening for us when we want them to. I am no exception to this; I have to recognize it and battle it constantly in life. If I want something, I simply have to go to the store or on-line and purchase it. I have to calm down about this and let this one go. I have no idea how far I am from Richmond, nor do I know how far I am from the finish line and I need to be okay with that. As a naturally anxious and somewhat A.D.H.D. individual, I have learned a few tools to channel my anxious behavior into construction actions. It's time to focus on the race at hand; calm down and above all focus on running on this road.

I start slowly eating some breakfast at my usual 80 miles per hour with half a stick of beef jerky, some coffee, water, trail mix and the other banana. And yes, I threw that peel into the trees on the side of the road. Technically I am sure it is littering but it's a banana peel. Let it return to the earth and let all the little creatures of the forest enjoy it as they want. I really start to wonder how Ella is doing. I am sure she is doing fine but again her lack of communication has my mind wondering. Usually she is so attentive to me, as if almost she had a 6th sense that tells her when I am thinking of her and when I would like to hear from her. I know, I have to put that out of my mind. Does it make me a bad boyfriend to NOT pull over and call her, or text her, or send her flowers via carrier pigeon? I always want to put people in front of myself so the answer is, my next stop I will walk around the gas station to get the blood flowing back into my legs and; give her a call. It seems a lot of people in relationships give each other all the attention they need within reason of work schedules and time out with other friends. My wife was always very good to me in this department, making sure she was usually home around the time I got home so I could see her and enjoy her company as I did until she was not there at all. I would still try to call her on her lunch break or after I got home just to enjoy the sound of her voice after she left and was asked not to call so much: lesson learned. My wife just could not stand me anymore as the person I was, so she left. Just because someone makes you happy does not mean you, make them happy. What a pleasure it was to communicate with that woman I married; happy or sad, laughing, crying or even yelling. Her attention always made me happy. I was the one to calm her mind and heart with my actions and words and enjoyed I could do that for her. As long as she had something to communicate with me, I always took it as a compliment. Damn, how I miss that woman. How I miss coming home to my funny little house with my son running out to greet me, jumping on the tank of my skoot as I rode it up the driveway. How I miss running around as Super Dad; dropping kids off and picking them up, volunteering for school functions, extracurricular activities and the like. Soccer and swimming with my son while marching band and roller derby with my teenage daughter. I could roll up in my Excursion, fill it with like-minded dads, hitch up a marching band trailer as we rolled to the next competition. Or I could fill it with roller derby ladies, turning down their sexual advances with a polite smile and get them all to the next bout. Damn I miss my kids. I miss them being so darn little, sometimes I forget to enjoy them as they are now.

"The night Max made mischief in his room of one kind, and another." I would bellow across the house and down the hall.

"Wait Daddy, I'm not ready yet, I'm still brushing my teef and finding my toto pajamas," my 5-year-old little girl would holler back to me. Then she climbed into bed, "Okay Daddy, I'm all ready for bed!" I would stomp into the room like a monster and read her favorite book of all, "Where the Wild Things Are," by Maurice Sendak.

In my funny little 'single young dad duplex' I rented at the time, I would pretend to read the book, simply flip through a page or two reciting the story from memory. My Pops read this book to me 1000 times and now I got to read it to her. It never took long for her to roll over and realize what I was doing. It was a great and funny game to play with her. Her beautiful eyes would look up at me, sighing, "Daddy, you are not reading the story, again!"

Retorting, I would say, "I am reading it sweetheart," as I smiled.

"But it's not the same Daddy, you have to read it from the pages," she would protest.

"As you wish Princess!" I would suffer my defeat from my little girl who obviously had me wrapped around her little finger. Finding my place in the book, "and now, let the wild rumpus begin! ROAR ROAR ROAR - ROAR ROAR ROAR - ROAR ROAR ROAR."

I can feel my eyes well up in tears as they slid out my goggles and down my cheeks into the wind. This racing stuff is cool but being a dad is still my favorite way to spend my time.

Sometimes I wish I had many more children, but I know the universe had a plan for me with the two I was blessed with. The fact that I could not keep their mothers around me long enough for either of my children to grow up in a happy, healthy, dual parent household is okay with me now. All my feelings on the 2 mothers of my 2 children have to be left out here in the wind. My lessons have been learned; life will need to move forward. My relationship with my children will always be what I make of it.

I need to concentrate more on the 'NOW' in their lives. Enjoy them for them, as them and not focus so much on the past. They are perfect just as they are and if I don't stop to enjoy them now, they will pass me by and the life we enjoy, and that is worth enjoying, will be wasted. Damn how I love those little monsters I have the pleasure to call my children.

#19

    I can feel it, I mean really feel it now. All is right with my world, my skoot is moving well. My children are healthy and so am I with the sun is in my face and wind against me. Oh, how I wish my son could see this, feel this and know this view and feeling; someday I hope he will. This is the type of view and feeling I remember while traveling with my Pops. The colors beam at me now like the skin on that perfect woman, the cool of a thousand kisses to my entire body, with all the smells the land and the earth has to offer. It's not something that can be recreated on any type of T.V. screen, it can only be here and now, a setting made by God and blessed upon me as the present, as it most definitely is a present indeed.

    My son and racing team crew chief is just the brightest light in my life. He is terribly in tune with me and the others around him who he loves. If I am ever down, getting antsy or anxious about something - I find him always playing cheering section for me and doing his best to lead me back into the bright light of life. This bright light in front of me on this road reminds me so much of him right now.

Allman Brothers, "Blue Sky," *Eat a Peach,* Capricorn Records, 1972

American Road Runner

Damn how my Pops used to love to sing this song when I was little. I know in this modern society of safety first and micromanagement of children it seems a little foolish to raise a boy around dangerous machines like these skoots. I can tell you it is just not my style to coddle or keep down what my son or daughter want to do. The only thing I fear for them more than dying is not living.

It took me a long time as a parent to learn how my son learns and how to teach him anything. When my daughter was a little girl, she just wanted to be good. She was always by my side with a big smile on her face and being a good girl. I don't remember ever having to scold her or tell her anything twice, she usually got it on the first request or example. My son, on the other hand, is a completely different story. As people we all have a few different ways we can learn. I am no expert at these items of psychology, and I want to be the best dad I can be for my kids but with my son - my best was just not good enough. I tried the usual of explaining, or leading by example but, that did not work. I tried a little banter or even scolding and that certainly did not work. Finally, when he was around two years old, I was preparing my outside grill for dinner. I opened the propane tank valve, turned on the flame valves and lit it up with that familiar click, click, click of the ignitor. Within a few seconds, my toddler of a boy came bouncing across the yard to see what the exciting click was about. He stopped, looked at me, looked at the grill, looked back at me as I said "HOT! Don't touch this son, it will burn you." He reached up his fat little right hand for the handle that was quick warming up. So, what did I do as dad? I could stop him, grab his arm or swat his hand away. Maybe pick him up and take him back across the yard to his Tonka truck and demand that he stays there. Well, instead I figured it won't kill him, so I stood there watching him as he got his pudgy little fingers around the handle then quickly let go. He looked at me and said "HOT," with big eyes of amazement.

"Yes son," I returned as he looked at his hand which was fine: just hot, not burned. Then he stood there and watched me as I prepped the grill, adding the chicken the whole time knowing he was cool to watch me, and we could hang out but not to touch because the grill was hot, and hot hurts.

The answer I found out was simple: my son does not learn by being told, he must experience everything himself to make his own observations and interpretations of what he wants to do and how he is going to do it. He is a thinker - not a follower. As he got older, I learned I could tell him phrases like: "Well you could jump off that tall building son but, you would die, and it's been nice knowing you kid." He stops, thinks and usually retorts with something like, "Okay dad". Imagine that, one of my offspring agreeing with me? I just had to figure out how to convince him to do so. Damn my little dude is awesome.

I can feel the weather warming up and quickly. Today, is going to be one of those hot and humid east coast days. Time to find the sun lotion and apply to my handsome face; again, and in a liberal fashion. From my paper maps point of view; I have to do this hooked curve over through Virginia then down to the Carolinas. I am not exactly sure where I am going but I have been there before. I have my map with hand scribbled directions that don't make much sense to me but as I already stated, that's half the adventure. Once I get past Richmond the roads should go down to a smaller interstate. It's gotta be less than 500 miles, and anyone can do that in half a day.

I'm in a bit of a strange place in my head and my body is close behind. Aches and pains have turned into simple switches that are keeping me awake, pissed off, and moving forward. The anxiety is slowly killing me to finish this race and the pain - damn the pain is so real, every part of my body just has a dull ache. The heat and humidity will be another factor to deal with. I had taken the gamble at the beginning of this race that I would be running in higher elevations and I had and set my carburetors up appropriately with a smaller or, leaner main jet. The skoot runs a lot better in the higher elevations as the air is a little thinner up there. With a little less fuel in the thinner air; the stoichiometry is closer to ideal mixture that is, air to fuel mixture ratio which with most petrol fuel sold in this country is somewhere around 14.7 parts air to 1-part fuel. I figured all this out by hooking my stoichiometry meter up to the skoot a few months ago then taking a nice ride up Big Bear Mountain; just an hour ride from my house. This was all to see how well it would do with these main jets at the higher elevations and my math was pretty right on. Down in Riverside at about 750 feet above sea level I only got about 15 to 1 but in the mountains at 6 or 7 thousand feet above sea level, I got a good 14 to 1. This was all at good cruising speeds and close enough for government work. The fuel air mixture analyzer I have is pretty versatile. Sometimes it really screws up and has to be reset but for the most part, I work with it and it has served me and all my skoots as needed. I hook it up with a cradle or wire frame I made for the sniffer that I can stuff in the back of the exhaust pipe the zip tie the wiring up the frame. I plug it into the battery then simply tape the digital read out to my bars and watch what's going on with the stoichiometries of whatever bike I am using it on. Yeah, it was made to be permanently mounted on a skoot but it's a couple hundred bucks so I only own one and move it around as needed. Besides; who needs to know the stoichiometry of their skoot all the time? I got a good base to run off, so I can simply make educated guesses from there.

If it gets too hot as I fall down in elevation, I'll be running lean and that could cause a whole bag of issues. Most notable, my engine parts could get way too hot, seize up and throw me arse handle over tea kettle. Yes, I brought extra jets and if I really think it is going to be an issue, I can pull over on the side of the road and have the new ones installed in half an hour or so. I would have to really want to do that to do that in my current reality. Usually it would not be a big deal, just some time, attention to detail. In my present state of mind and lack of sleep, it may take might take me almost an hour. Also, I could really slip with a screwdriver, or break the throttle cable, or who knows what as my hands are just not working correctly at this present time. This vibrating, sucker punching machine of mine has been dishing out all sorts of havoc to my body. Sometimes in life when you just are not sure what to do; it's best to do nothing at all. That may work for now, but I am sure eventually today I will have to address this carb issue. I better start formulating a plan in my head.

It's time to stop again. I am not in Richmond yet, but I can feel myself getting closer. The pines are starting to really lineup thicker and thicker now. I find a good-looking petrol place and pull off. Dirt lot and all, it looks like an old convenience store off the side road of the side road but it's got pumps so it will work. I pull up to a pump and throw the kickstand down with my boot, then fall off the skoot - literally. I climb up off the ground and slowly but surely remove my vest, then jacket, helmet, goggles and gloves. Grabbing my coffee tumbler, it's time for coffee and some real breakfast like a muffin or cinnamon roll. Slide my card and it's declined. This happens a lot with how fast I move so I bring out the other card as I carry 2 just for this reason. No matter how many times I have chatted with a customer rep from one of those credit-card companies, they just don't get it that I travel, and travel fast. The cards able me to pay for gas quicker, and hotel rooms as a good third-party insurance. Other than that, I prefer to pay cash. I pump, then the caps go back on. The station is almost empty, so I leave the skoot in front of the pump. Walking to the store now and dammit; I am really having walking issues. My legs feel like they are not even there. No one part of them hurt they just don't want to work right now. I have to stop and think only to remember I did not perform any skootin' yoga in the last few hours. Let's walk around the gas station for a minute my dear legs; shall we. I walk, I stretch my calves on the curb, I pull up my overalls and squat and fall over. F.Y.I. gravel hurts a lot more than asphalt when ya fall on it. Damn, I need to get this straight and manage this better if I am going to finish this race! Shame on me for my poor treatment of something so important like the health and flexibility of my sexy dad bod. Standing up now, slowly but surely; moving more of my body now and getting it done.

I walk into the convenience store to find a few of the civilian crowd and local taxpayers staring at me. I say good morning and turn for the coffee paying them no mind. They all seem like simple folk who are just confused or maybe curious about my freak flag flying as high as it does to people such as them. Coffee: black today, Gatorade, water, oh a banana nut muffin, sunflower seeds but damn; no fresh fruit. I go up to pay and have to manage around the small crowd. I have seen this movie before, this is where they either say hello or simply try to beat the shit out of me. The cashier rings me up and I pay with cash. I slip back through the crowd nodding with my big smile and wish them all a good day. I return to the skoot and can see a man staring out the window; damn, this could be bad. "The man is at the window; the man is at the window" I have to give it all over to the universe at this point and just accept... whatever. Stowing my goods in my tank bag then adorning my gear. I straddle my machine and decide to change goggles to another tinted pair. My face has started to chafe so my face and I are hoping this other pair will chafe in a different place. I would hate to show too much chafing on my handsome mug, so I apply a little chap stick to said mug and hope for the best. I start up and motor away as casually as can be, it's time to get running again.

With a cough and wheeze this old cop skoot fires to life ready to eat up more road. Slowly I motor out the parking lot, turning my head as I go with a smile and a wave to all the pretty customers still staring at me through the window. Damn, did I fuck one of their daughters the wrong way at some point in my past? It always amazes me how some people just can't let people be people. I reckon they'll be telling this story at the local bar for a month, with a few embellishments of how they 'scared' the dirty biker out of town.

#20

The problem with a mind like mine is sometimes it wanders into the bad places. Sometimes I let the mistakes of misfortunes that have plagued me in the past creep back up on me; a bad habit to say the least. At my age, or in what society will sometime refer to as 'middle age', I have seen and experienced a few things regarding relationships with other people. Whether business or intimate, I am always cautious at anything that comes too easy or too hard. The ability to filter through all of this crap and keep myself happy has always been a challenge to say the least. Emotional issues and the management of said issues have always been hard in my family. Personally, it took the act of my wife leaving me for a spark to ignite in my brain. I was not a drunk or a bum, nor an abuser, or anything that society or I could point at and blame for my wife leaving. At the end of the day; she just needed to be without me, we had grown apart and her idea of happiness in a relationship with another human being no longer included me. The best relationship advice I received consisted of the reminders from my friends and family that I am a person of worth and value. Just because my wife did not see it or was not interested in it did not mean it was not there. I just had to push through all the bullshit in my mind and be okay with me, being me. In my new relationship, I have been able to move a few things around. If she does not want to talk to me or is not available; I have learned to be okay with that. If she needs time with her family or time with her friends, by all means; have at it lady. If in the end she decides she doesn't want me, well that sucks but so be it. I've got a house to run, kids to raise, a career to work and a lifestyle of relaxing wrenching, riding and racing to partake in. Lucky me to get to enjoy her and lucky her to get to enjoy me. No matter what my mind wants to tell me as right or wrong, I know I can separate my feelings from my mind and right now, no matter how much pain I am in; I will be thankful for it as it is keeping me going here on my chosen road in this race - in this life. I mean it's not like I am flying through outer space in a spaceship built by the lowest government bidder… I am not on fire or anything so all will be okay. Of course, I was on fire a few days ago though…

Friday night before this race started, when the family and I were on the playas of El Mirage, my good friend Jake The Flying Dutchman pulled into camp where Ella and I were hanging out with our friends Matt and Twila. Twila is the cool photographer who makes me and my skoots look as righteous as humanly possible and then some. As Jake pulled in, I could sense him and Twila had something planned as he quickly laid out a plethora of items purchased at the discount store. None of it made much sense to me so I bid them all a good night as they both turned to me and informed me, they were going to do a photoshoot and my skoot and I were the models. Okay, I wondered, how this is going to go?

Jake had me move the skoot 30 or so feet out onto the dark racecourse where he had me sit on the skoot. Then, with the camera on a tripod, Twila yelled "GO!" Jake, proceeded to light up and swing behind me a small rope, tied to a metal whisk stuffed with steel wool that was soaked in lubricant and lit on fire. I sat there motionless as I heard Jakes arm sucking wind behind me and, fire raining down on my skoot and I. I had to trust he knew what he was doing or that he had done this before, which it turned out he had not. The outcome was a brilliant time lapse picture of my skoot with me upon it and a round force of fire behind us that raining down like a waterfall of awesomeness. Wow these friends of mine know how to make me look cool and scare the crap out of me all at the same time. Lucky me.

I have gotten to Richmond and taken Interstate 95 south where I will soon find the 64W and take that south to Highway 1 and into the town of Southern Pines, North Carolina to finish at the Best Western Hotel. Soon the course will start to divert off the interstates and onto the black or blue highway. The temperature and humidity are rising. I can feel it, and I mean: REALLY, FEEL IT! My mind has been racing around this subject for several minutes. Maybe it's just my lack of personal hygiene? Maybe it's my lack of acclamation to the humid weather of the south here? I have to ponder and concentrate on this very hard. I have a problem, I think, and I need to come up with a solution and fast. After several days without appropriate sleep, the mind has joined the body in rebelling against my want and desire to move forward. Slowly but surely, this hot scorching southern sun beating down can cause me, and more importantly my machine, a lot of problems; even failure.

Jimi Hendrix "Who Knows" *Band of Gypsys (Live At Fillmore East, New York)* Capitol Records, 1970.

As far as my hygiene is concerned, it has been a few days since I have showered and I can really smell the sweat in my hair wrap, gross as gross can be but all part of it. It is certain that everything will feel a little hotter than it should as my wind beaten clothing is certainly saturated in all the manly sweat it could ever absorb off of my skin. In the wind at this speed, it all seems to evaporate leaving behind a rough buildup of salt and odor, fluttering and beating against my skin. The chaffing will soon be a problem, but I have to embrace it for now as I can feel the finish line in front of me. I realize that a little pain will not slow me down but, in fact, the pain and discomfort from the chafing heat on certain parts of my body that I did not know even existed will aid my current quest against every fiber in my body's want to just fucking stop and lay down. It will all annoy me and my being to no end and the only solution now is, FINISH THIS FUCKING RACE!!!

I take my left glove off my hand with my teeth stowing it between my cock and the seat. I reach out to the sky slowly and feel the heat in the wind that beats against my hand. I reach down to the road and the engine; all is hot, hotter than it should be maybe or just hotter than I ever remember it being. It's not me; it's the heat. This heat is going to kill my skoot if I let it. The middle of nowhere is about my location, somewhere in the state of Virginia or maybe North Carolina, at this point I am just not sure. I need a few things, and I need to get to work fast and efficiently, with my body and mind in this current state of bogglery. I am not sure exactly what that word bogglery means but it sounds extremely appropriate right about now. My glove goes back on my hand.

After slowing down my pace and my engine, I am confident in my bogglery state that I have a plan. I start looking; looking and searching the sides of the road for a small town. Somewhere with an auto parts store and a gas station, preferably next to each other. Maybe a diesel mechanic's shop attached to a large big rig servicing convenient store. I need a shade tree as well but that should not be a problem, there are trees everywhere in this part of the world. Big arse trees that line the road like our man-made walls on the Southern California freeways. The problem sticks me like a match; I am not in my most known, comfort zone. If I was riding through the California desert or anywhere in the southwest, I would know most places. Most small towns, even most large truck stops that seem to make themselves small towns. I would have memories of being there as a young boy with my Pops. I would feel and know comfort in the barren desert landscape but here; here it is all strange and new to me. The answer is people need things. People like me built these roads and this infrastructure so, eventually, with a little patience I will find what I am looking for no matter how strange the current scenery may be. It is all America and all for me.

It's been several miles and I see nothing that makes sense to me for what I need. Moving slowly as I am is really trying my patience but what choice do I have right about now. Then, I see what appears to be an older style business frontage road with gas station and several food signs on the large roadway placards. One of them I miss as I am passing the big rigs, damn those cargo trailers make for terrible windows. This unfortunately happens often with my life in the fast lane. Even at my slower than usual speed right now, I still find big rigs moving much slower than me. And as usual, when it's time to pass one, the sequence is long and drawn out and right now it seems to take forever. I look in my rear-view mirror for traffic, look over my left shoulder for traffic, then move the skoot to the right side of the right lane to see ahead and make sure I won't miss any large marker signs. Then the mirror again, then over my shoulder again, then pass the dang big rig. This all takes less than 3 seconds but, it needs to be done this way just for this exact reason - I hate it when I miss roadway signage. That signage was placed there just for me, to inform me and when I miss it, I am left uninformed and sniffing with my nose in hopes of finding what I need.

Passing and pulling back right to the slow lane, then the off ramp, turn right and slow down on a business frontage road and crap, nothing. Looking to my left I can still see the interstate every now and then, peeking and winking at me through the monster trees. I know above all I must not lose that damn interstate, or I will have to turn around and damn; I do not ever want to have to turn around - like ever!!!

Allman Brothers, "Sweet Melissa" *Eat a Peach,* Capricorn Records, 1972.

It always seems to take a lifetime when one is hoping and/or wishing for something to appear. For some reason the idea that 50 other people are on this road and racing me only seems to compound this lifetime of waiting for what I need right now! This is simple anxiety, and this is simply one of those times. The fear that what I want will not be there as I expect it to be. I am very aware of this anxiety and even in my current state of 'fuck it all race mode,' I can and will curb it. I mumble to myself; "If you cannot find what you are looking for, it is okay, you will find it farther down the road, it's just time and patience you impatient bastard Bob." Reassuring myself that the fear of the unknown or the future is not valid. I rummage in the top of my tank bag and grab a smoke and hit the lighter, concentrating on it popping back up, light my smoke and drag. "This is a road; other people exist and live here so why not you Bob? Enjoy this road sir, soon it will all be over, and you are going to miss this."

Damn it is beautiful out here, just trees and green, as far as the eye can see. Finally, up ahead, I start to see structures and like a gift from the heavens a gas station appears, but it's a small one and it may not serve me as I need it too. Another mile of road goes under my tires then, I see an old school Napa Auto Parts store complete with gas station across the street. I pull into the station's white fine gravel lot. There is a large tree throwing shade in the corner, I feel like I have won the lottery as my body breathes a sigh of relief.

#21

Nobody wants to use the restroom with greasy hands - or do they?

My schooling taught me to educate myself, get good grades and I won't have to get my hands dirty to make a living. Most of my elementary years were spent in private Catholic school where I was happy to run from dirt, always wanting to keep my uniform crisp and clean and above all, my tie perfect. As I got older, I learned very quickly that you just don't get much done keeping your damn hands clean. If you want something to live, something else has to die and the cleanliness of my hands is a good place to start. Die cleanliness die. It seems that until 100 years ago, men were given prestige and glory from society on how many fingers they were missing. The more fingers lost; the harder you worked and more you must have earned from your hard work. These days it seems nothing can be farther from that truth. If a man is missing a digit or two, he must have done something wrong so there must be something wrong with him. I personally like the older theory; if you are a man who can work with his hands, you got my vote. There is a ton of unseen education in all things manual these days that most do not stop and comprehend. If you needed your driveway laid in brick for example, the average American of today will hire someone to do it under to false statements of 'not having enough time or having enough money to pay someone else to do it'. Under a similar regime of thinking, my 'Baby Boomer Generation' Pops used to say: "You can't beat a man at his own game. His specialty is what he does, and he will - do it better than you."

This statement might be true Pops but, "Watch me compete!" So, my Pops would watch, always being there to add his fatherly advice and get in my way about it. As I mentioned, he is the laziest, most creative man I have ever known. He will always let his mind find the easiest way of doing something, usually about the time I have ran circles around something to get it done. With his age and very engineering mind, comes a lot of wisdom, but his attitude of 'hiring someone else to do for him' will never be my style.

Slowly but surely, I killed the spoon feed ideology handed to me by so many educators and adults. I will be getting my hands dirty to earn a living, I will be washing my hands before I use the restroom - as well as after. Yes, a little lotion to the hands is okay but at the end of the day there might be grease and dirt under my fingernails and embedded in the calluses. It's just my reality - where I am comfortable. Oh, I can still wear a suit and tie a tie thanks to my Pops but the blue color I put on every day suits me just fine. Right now, it is time to get my hands dirty and place them in small places to exercise some of my mechanical trades, both romantic and classical. I know some people shy away from owning or working on Japanese motorcycles because they do not like all the small spaces you have to get your fingers into. Personally, I like to pride myself on getting my thick manly fingers into small places; all puns intended so here goes nothing.

I pull to a pump, fall off my machine letting the pump catch me and slowly work my way to a standing position. As usual my saddle rag falls over and hits the oily greasy concrete and I get to bend over to pick it up. Card out, swipe, tank bag undone I start to fill. Then of course, button all of that up and move to the front tank - undoing the netting and my bag hits the concrete. I get to pick that up and redoing and securing all as needed. I learned a long time ago to never leave anything undone on my skoot, anywhere, at any time - that's how shit flies off in the wind. All the same old familiar routine that I rebuilt and engineered for this machine. I pull the receipt, place it in my handy sophisticated filling system known as the sandwich bag in my inner vest pocket then, head inside grabbing my tumbler on the way. It is hot, like Texas hot and humid as fuck. Stretching all I can in my body as I walk; I grab 2 Gatorade bottles, 2 water bottles, refill my coffee cup for some strange reason in this heat and go to the clerk. It takes me a few minutes in line as there are several people in front of me which I don't really mind as it is nice and cool inside here. I seem to be making everyone a little nervous with my pirate attire. I just smile at all those who I meet eyes with and keep a cheery all though be it; tiresome outlook. Paying the clerk, he starts chatting with me asking me how my day is and all the regular questions. We chat for a brief moment about the humid weather and the forecast of hotter weather then; I'm back outside in the thick of it. It was odd but he seemed friendlier with me than the other customers, maybe he secretly wants to dress like a pirate too?

I stow or load my newly found consumables on my skoot, mostly in my front netting. Pushing the machine across the parking lot to a nice shade tree I see over by the air machine. A group of young men from a car at the pumps run over to assist me. I accept their help and we get the machine the 20 yards or so into the shade. I thank them and wave as they start to play the classic game of 20 questions. Conceding to all their wonder; I admit to them that the machine is not broken, I am simply moving it out of the way and enjoy the exercise of pushing it to keep the blood flowing in my legs. They scratch their heads as I have a good laugh about it all, claiming my old age as the reason and, bid them good day. It takes a few moments but eventually they walk back to their car. It's not that I don't want them to know that I am about to take my carbs off, it's just I don't always feel like explaining my mechanical thinking to everyone. I have learned the hard way over the years that when I talk shop with most, they rarely follow what I am saying. This can lead to a heated match of explaining myself and right now in this heat - I'm going to avoid all that at almost any cost. It's my fault mostly as I just don't formulate very well my explanations, my left-handed - right brain self is just different than most.

It always seems the more questions I personally have on things, the more I answer them and the more I answer them; the more questions l have. It's a song as old as time that goes around and around in my longing for knowledge, I sometimes overlook a very important ideology I have learned. It is simple; 'I can own something, or it can own me'. I may own this machine or my house and the land it sits upon but at the end of the day; these things will still be here when I am gone. If I should die on this road today, all this stuff will still existence. I am really just part of its life, for this moment in time. It is all materials thrown together to make something that means something to us human beings. My skoot moves me, forward down this road at great speed as my house keeps me warm and dry and gives me somewhere to put all my stuff. This ideology took me a long time to recognize and exercise, my use of it is not perfect and I suspect I will get better at using it in the future; I hope. I have learned to refer to it all as; my relationship with stuff. Just simple ideology that we, as humans, own stuff. It does not own us unless we allow it too, and we get to make all our stuff our bitch and just fucking own it.

    Squatting next to my skoot, the hand tools needed come out of the saddlebags that hang under the seat. My favorite Phillips screwdriver, a flathead screwdriver and my little baggy of extra jets all gets scattered on top of my seat. The flathead is employed to remove my quad or 4 air filters that adorn the back side of the carburetors. I can access 2 from one side of the skoot then the other 2 from the other side. Setting them on the ground next to me, I can't help but notice how caked they are with dirt; evenly but, good and dirty. I cleaned them before I left on this race, but I must of ridden through a dust storm at night or something and not noticed. These particular types of filters are washable and reusable, and made in my hometown of Riverside. I can wash them in the bathroom sink then re oil them as I did remember to bring some air filter oil, but they would need some time to dry in the sun. For right now I am going to set them aside.

    I handle the Phillips next and unscrew the clamps that hold the carbs to the back or front of the engine. The engine is actually backwards in these old kz1000 Kawasaki, like most skoots. That is, the front or intake of the engine faces the back while the back or exhaust side of the engine faces to the front. The carbs pull off with some strong arming, but I get them to pop out of the boots that hold them to the engine. I have done this many times before, so I better be a damn expert. The engine is hot and working hard to burn me, almost in anger, for all I have put it through in the last 50 hours. I have to pull the throttle cable off the set of carbs as well. This is always a little tricky in its small space but a lot easier to pull off then put back on.

With my carbs now off the engine and in my hands; I secure myself between the tree and the skoot and take a look around to make sure no one is paying me too much attention. Quickly glancing at the station pumps and the few people walking in and out of the convenience store it occurs to me that they all seem to be glancing at me. I do a double take and realize I, am the only white person here at this gas station. I do not think this is a problem or issue however, I am not too sure; this is not my side of the country. I'm honestly not even sure what state I am in right now. I may or may not be making these people feel nervous with my actions hanging out next to this tree and ripping my motorcycle apart in this parking lot. Well, my carbs are out, best to move forward. No one seems to have their eyes on me right now so off to the side of the skoot the carbs go upside down spilling several ounces of fuel onto a rag I have set on the ground. Sitting with my legs crossed to keep myself low behind the bike; the carbs sit in my lap. I make quick work of pulling the bowls off the carbs with the several turns of my screwdriver on each of the 4 screws that secure the bowl to the carb. 4 cylinders on this machine means 4 carbs all secure together which equals 16 screws to be loosened and turned. I pull the bowls off and place the screws in them, keeping them in order, right in front of me on the ground. With the flathead screwdriver, I slowly and gingerly remove all 4 of the main jets smiling up at me; one per carb. I hold them up to the light and can see they are all clean, free from obstruction. From my baggy of jets, I pull a quad set of 120 jets only to realize; I only have 3 of the 4 jets that I need. I check again and again in this little plastic sandwich bag and of course, it has developed a small hole and after a quick inventory, it seems one is missing. I can assume the small jet is in my saddle bag however, I kept these jets in the spare parts saddle bag which is on the other side, or right side, of the skoot and I am currently comfortable cross legged and hidden on the left side of the machine; damn.

Setting the carbs on the ground almost under the skoot, I slowly pull myself up and this is not working. My legs are just not having it. Damn this is a problem on top of a problem, and it needs to be figured out quickly. I start to roll on my butt a little to the left and to the right; damn this must look ridiculous. Stopping for a moment, I pick up my coffee tumbler and take a swig, crap that's hot, and it's hot; all this is adding up... trying my patience. "Go Bob, Go! Do This Bob - Do This! Take your time in a hurry and get this done!" I repeat to myself several times before gritting through the pain and rolling over to one leg slowly pulling myself up. Fuck it hurts but I don't want to be here anymore! I am up, I think, standing with my legs straight and back bent as my body is bending over the skoot, resting my forearms on the seat. I open the right-side saddle bag in front of me now and remove its contents of spare parts and put them into this bag. My body groans back at me as I lay so much of its weight on my chest and lungs. It is a good thing I have not eaten much at this point as I am sure I would be throwing up right about now as being stopped this long is starting to make me sick. Slowly, all the items come out as I dig and dig; looking for the lost shiny golden jet. The saddle bag, is now empty and my missing jet, is nowhere to be found. Out of sheer frustration; I rummage around the tank bag only to find an extra plastic bag I would usually put on my feet. I unfold it as it is folded into a ridiculously small ball my girlfriend Ella likes to fold these things into. Not going to assist me now in this.

By now, my legs are getting some blood flow in them, so I straighten. I have a small problem on my mind and in my hands that I need to figure out. Maybe I could just run 2 larger jets on the inner cylinders as they tend to run hotter? Well it's an idea. Slowly and with great purpose trying not to trip on myself, I move to the other side of the skoot and with my tail between my legs, I accept the defeat of my situation and start repacking the right-side saddle bag. Putting the contents now in the plastic bag, because why not, and repacking them all as organized as possible. The spare clutch cable goes in first, then the small case of fuses, tire valves, safety wire, bolts and nuts and other weird odds and ends goes in next. Then I pull the spare coil complete with wires and set it in only to hear something hit the pavement. Closing my eyes and keeping my head straight, I do my best to have an audible memory. I heard something hit the ground but did not see it. Which way did it go? I point a few degrees to the right underneath me and see nothing. Slowly getting back down on my knees I see a lot of carbs and parts under my skoot on the black rocky asphalt parking lot. I start moving everything around and there it is, like a shiny gold tooth staring at me from under one of the carbs; my missing jet. Burning my arm on the exhaust pipe a little and... "gotcha." Trying to stand up but, once again, cannot. I throw the jet in my mouth so as not to lose it again and start rocking my body to throw a leg up and get off my knees. Slowly I do this and start walking. I don't care where I am walking just in a small circle around my machine to get the blood flowing again. After a few good back and forth walks in the parking lot and around the skoot a few times, I sit back down on the left side of my machine to attend to the business at hand. I feel better, Mr. Left and Mr. Right leg are not fighting so much. It always amazes me what a good walk can do for my body. It's something my Pops taught me and today, it worked well. Pops has several health issues like asthma and diabetes, but he rarely lets those issues slow him down. When we stop to fuel we walk, if only for a few minutes, around the parking lot.

The jet spits out of my mouth and into my hand, 1,2,3,4. I have them all now, all size 120 little shiny main jets. Double checking the very small imprint on the tops of them, I confirm and am back in business. The set of carbs return to my lap and in the jets go. I double check the floats and other components of the bowls on the carbs and all seems fine. This does not necessarily mean that all is fine, but all looks fine so if the 'God of Speed' is smiling down on me; all should be good. The bowl gaskets are aligned and one by one the bowls go back on as I tighten the screws in a star fashion to keep the gasket seated well. I hold the carbs up and do a quick inspection of them from all angles - all looks good. The butterflies and throats of the carbs are a little dirty but that's to be expected after 2,500 miles on them. The filters are terribly dirty and some of that fine engine killing dust is working its way through the air filters. I carry some Q-tips in my personal kit so that's now what I need in my worn-out hands.

Moving my left arm to undo the net on the front of the bike, the bag comes crashing down next to me. Positioning it correctly; I unzip it and retrieve my personal dopp kit and the Q-tips within it, all pretty and lined up in their own little travel case. Grabbing a few, I start dipping them in the small puddle of gas I left in my rag on the blacktop. I hold the carbs in my lap so I can open the butterflies with one hand while I reach in there with the wet, gas-soaked Q-tips with the other hand. Slowly the black grit and dust removes itself from the carbs throat and the butterflies and soaks into the Q-tips.

As I sit there performing this, I have to stop and ask myself: why? Why am I really worried about this, right now? I suspect most would simply throw the carbs back on the skoot and get down the road but here I am: in the middle of a race, on the side of the road in a gas station parking lot, lacking sleep and cleaning my carbs. It seems this is something very small and like a ticker in my head the dinger goes off and reminds me of many memories of people simply getting pissed off at me for little stunts like this. My ex-wife especially was good at reminding me I was missing managing something if I took a few extra minutes to make it right for me. Not right or wrong in general; just right for me. My coworkers, siblings, peers, most adults; they would all be frustrated to no end at actions like this. To me, myself and I; this and these actions of mine are what make me, well; me. I am doing this my way, to my level of comfort, as a free tax paying American and there is no one around to stop me. It's time to button this up and get back in this race.

Like a long sang song on my tongue, I get the carbs back in and with a bit of luck and skill, the throttle cable hooks back up without too much hassle with a special tool I have remade for this purpose. Wow, that was weird; usually it's several minutes of fuss but the 'God of Speed' seems to be on my side with this one. All gets quickly packed back on the machine in its proper place, my gear goes back on and my air filters get stashed in my oil bag; I'll just go without those for now.

I adorn my gear and the skoot roars to life on the first hit of the switch after a little priming of fuel in the carbs. I go to pull out then stop myself. Put it in neutral, jump off, take one more walk around and double check everything. This is usually where something would be left undone or open and fly out or off the skoot down the road, but all is right. I double check my gear and all is right, damn I am getting good at this, whatever this skill actually is. Saddling up and off I go, through the few lights and stop signs of the little town I still don't know the name of and notice my throttle position is very different than it was before. That is; 1/4 throttle is now 1/8 throttle. With a little twist of my right hand, I get a big response. That's okay for now - it will have to do. I can manage this as long as I place my right thumb sideways on the throttle housing at low speeds... done. This machine has a lot of horsepower and I feel it trying to dump me as I feather the big, hard clutch. None of this will matter in a mile as the machine and I get back on the only known mistress of mine; the road.

Alien Ant Farm, "Movies," *Greatest Hits,* Chick Music Records, 1999

#22

Running again, just my machine and I. The heat is great and gaining, but I don't need to care about that so much at this point. This mighty cop chop #27 between my legs is rocking it; pulling strong and keeping up with my throttle hand. I have done all I can do to make sure it will make it in this heat, the rest is up to the machine and the universe. With steady purpose, the road beneath my feet reminds me that we are simply flying over it with inches to spare. Hitting the 64w, time is running out and the finish line is getting near. I forgot to pee at the last stop, too much else going on, emptying my bladder got forgotten - again. Damn how I hate to stop just too pee. I could just pee my pants or hang my cock out in the wind and let it go but I have heard from other Stampeders that this causes a lot more mess on everything you own instead of just your pants. I wait a few minutes; flying around the big rigs and other slower moving vehicles. Using it all like an arcade game to keep my mind awake and body from falling asleep. Like a gift a rest stop appears, I must have missed the signage somewhere behind me. We hit the off ramp, quickly.

Pulling in next to a few other motorcycles, I dismount as graciously as possible amongst the picnicking citizens with children playing. All are enjoying the warm afternoon under the shade trees. I walk uphill to the restrooms and have developed a new theory; anywhere other than the southwest, all rest stops in this country are situated on a hill, ya have to walk up or down to get to the restrooms. I pee and actually find soap to wash my hands while throwing some water on my face. Damn I can feel all the oil and dirt making one hell of a mess on my handsome mug. In my current condition this all takes one hell of an effort. When I reach my skoot several men in riding vests are pointing and conversing over my machine. I assume they all ride the skoots I parked next too but these days, ya never know as I have seen a ton of weirdos wearing riding vests while driving cars.

"Good Morning," I say to them as best I can.

"Good Afternoon," one of them responds with a smile on his face. Racing East has left me with a sense of time that's way off. I have lost 3 hours, in my mind, it's 9 in the morning, here it's noon already.

"Are you one of those Stampeders?" another one asks.

"I am, where are you guys heading to?"

"Same place you are, only we are planning to get there tomorrow or, maybe the next day. We are whatcha might refer to as 'Long Roaders,' that is how 'L-O-N-G' can we take to get there, types. Y'all left California a few days ago?"

"Sunday; yes Sir,"

Our conversation is cut off by the roar of some engines behind me. I spin around to the road and catch a glimpse through the trees of 2 of my competitors flying fast by.

"Those look like some of your fellow racers passing you by, ya best get your hustle on there, young man!"

I look at my skoot as all these kind gentlemen jump out of my way. With a vengeance I mount; helmet, gloves and start it to life. "Look me up at the show when ya get there gentlemen. Enjoy your road!" I yell over my shoulder.

I back out and take off with cheers from all those men around me. Hauling arse, I hit the road, knowing damn well I won't catch up with these 2 corn feed Iowa boys on their old chops. They have new V-twin engines in those things and damn those machines of theirs look sweet and sound mean. All I need them to do is stop for a smoke or a food break and I will put myself in front of them. I don't think they saw me so my plan may work especially if I don't catch them out here. If they glimpse me at all, my plan will be fouled. They will take off and we will all be on the evening news doing 120 mph to the finish line. Nothing seems to wake me up like a little competition. Seeing fellow competitors sure did get my blood pumping again.

It slowly occurs to me I have not heard my phone go off lately. Then I realize I am not exactly sure where my phone is. It's not in its case or clipped on top of my tank bag. I feel on my hip; no, not there as I am wearing my overalls. Maybe in my vest somewhere? I feel around but can't feel anything. Did I lose my phone? That would suck!

I stop looking for a minute, I just don't have the energy for this right now. If my phone is lost; so be it. I'll find another one on the other side. After several minutes I reach for a smoke but can't find those either. Wow; everything is lost out here but me. Wait; am I on the right road? The question is real as it enters my mind. After a few more miles, a small off ramp then on ramp appear out here in this green jungle then, a road or route marker sign. Yes, I am on the right road, so everything IS lost but me. Waiting for a straight stretch of road; I open my tank bag again, a little more this time, and very slowly as to not spill its contents out to the wind. I take my left glove off with my right hand and keep the glove between my right hand and throttle. Rummaging around in my tank bag for my smokes, I find all my goggles, glasses, some breath mints, phone, a banana but nothing I can smoke. I pull my hand out defeated and bummed. Leaning the skoot and I take a few sucker punches from the road. I wait patiently to reach back into my tank bag only to have it occur to me; my phone is in there and that was one of the items I was looking for I think, but I don't remember why. After several minutes, I get the opportunity and reach back in, grabbing my phone and stowing it in my upper vest pocket. After a few more minutes, there is still no luck with the smokes. The pack is yellow, and even after a few glances I cannot find it. I have packs of smokes stowed all over this machine and have unfortunately gone through a few. I just can't remember where I would have stowed them right about now. I am left to calm down; chewing on sunflower seeds and sipping my coffee, although it is tasting weird right about now.

Pulling out my phone to fuss with; I can see it is totally offline, like there is no service out here. After another 20 miles or so, I look at it again and it is still offline. I hit the power button and have to assume it has an issue. It slowly lights back up and starts going crazy, apparently it has been offline most of the morning, or maybe since last night. Now I know why I have not heard from Ella in a while. It seems everyone these days is sold that communication is safety; lucky for the communication companies as they are always coming out with a new device to sell me to keep me 'safe'. My time with my phone off had to be the best time in this race. Safety is purely a state of mind in my opinion. By opinion, I mean it's all opinion, safety is pure opinion but, if I run from technology I know it will chase me so here I am, with a bitchin' new cell phone, enjoying all it has to offer, maybe even a little safety. It is nice to know I can call someone if all else fails but knowing my luck, I would blow up my engine out of cell tower range and have to rely on the people of the land around me. I reply back to Ella with a pic of myself then ignore the rest of the notifications; I have a race to finish.

#23

I'm gonna have to make one more fuel stop before this race is over, maybe this side of Raleigh, North Carolina so I don't get too far away from civilization and the gas stations on the other side of that big city. There is a lot of country out here and wow have the states been flying by lately. I have been looking forward to this last stop for a long time. There's one; it will do, almost on top of the road. These quick stop, overhead gas stations out here are really cool and kind of a novelty to a westerner like me. I pull off and do the usual only pull my goggles off and won't put them back on; into my tank bag they go. Instead I will shed them and my face shield and enjoy my sunglasses the last hundred plus miles. The ache in my head and ringing in my ear is very real, the wind in my face will be a welcome change to the closed in feeling of goggles and face shield. I check my oil and it's really low, like almost a quart, way beneath my comfort level and the comfort level of the skoot I am sure... dammit Bob!

This heat is really playing its part on this poor machine of mine. Maybe I've been neglecting the oil level the last few hundred miles? Time to do my best to make it right. Pushing the skoot from pump to parking stall, I start to marvel at how well this machine is doing. I stop and look it over and all seems good and for some strange reason, clean - just shiny all over. All that rain a few states back really did a job. I would never waste time cleaning or polishing this machine to this type of luster. My coffee tumbler is full of burnt coffee. I picked it up at the last stop and can't blame them, after all it's hot out here. I am sure I'm the only one buying coffee at gas stations today. I take the cup in for a refill and find a sink next to the island of coffee dispensers. I wash my cup in the sink as it is caked with grease, debris, old dried up coffee and road dirt. Shutting off the water; I graze my hand on the spout and cut myself. My finger is busy bleeding itself out, all over the sink and floor. Lucky for me, there is a sink. I wash my finger then wrap it in my headwrap. Hopefully the clerk will just think I am hanging on to it and not bleeding all over their store. I get more coffee cursing myself a little; I mean who needs coffee now? I am sure I do not, but this is habit, simply feeding my habit of getting coffee at a stop. I clean up my blood mess with some paper towels, fill my tumbler with coffee and ice, grab some mini donuts because damn I have earned them, then several water bottles and pay. Oh, and I buy two extra packs of smokes just in case.

    I run out and stow everything everywhere I can. My body is moving for me but much slower than usual. Laboring to do anything has become a huge chore, like 10-fold. I stow my face shield in my back-side bag that started this race full of treats and a soft case for my face shield but can't find that. It must have fallen out somewhere, so a soft towel and a plastic bag will have to do. I am tempted to polish the bugs off before stowing it but that will have to wait. Open my other bag, get all the oil stuff out and fill the engine, then a few shots of wax on the chain and all should be good. My rear tire's bald spot is getting bigger but at this point, I'm just gonna have to hope it holds.

    After putting my earbuds in and helmet on, I think I hear talk about my cop chop, and that can't be right. I look around and can see two guys talking about my machine, but from ten feet away. I stop and have to really concentrate on them to hear what they are saying. They are complimenting my type of engine; it all seems like a dream right about now in my haze. Then they start to compliment me on how clean and well-polished my skoot is. I smile and laugh to myself as I labor to remember to breathe. I agree with them, thank them, and throw down my kickstand. Jumping off the skoot; I try to make it to a trash can but cannot, instead I find a planter, fall to my knees and puke. The men are terribly confused by this, but I know exactly what it is, my land sickness has taken over and my body is mad and confused at being stopped for so long. I walk back to them with an embarrassed look on my face; grab my water and start to wash out my mouth; swishing, spitting and smiling. The men walk away waving goodbye; well that was nice of them. I honestly assumed I would have a peanut gallery of questions after my puking stunt but, they walked away as true gentlemen should, or maybe I just scared them off.

Go Bob, GO!!! I don my simple cool aviator sunglasses and mount up. With the sun in the west sky I ride off and through this big confusing white concrete of a parking lot, twice. I cannot find the damn on ramp in the direction I need to be traveling to save my life... Damn I am so uncool right about now and must look stupid as hell.

Highwaymen, "Highway Man," *Highwaymen.* Columbia Nashville, 1985

Why am I out here killing myself on this road - on this on this damn machine? I could be home, enjoying the spoils of my hard work. Comfortable in my big leather chair watching a cool old VHS tape in the player with my phone in hand checking my social media status every 5 minutes. The air conditioning blasting in my face while I sip cool coffee and indulge myself in a cool old western novel, enjoying blow jobs and sandwiches from Ella. Oh, sure there will be common birthday parties and other social gatherings to get me out of the house every once and while but someday, I need to slow down. I need to get off this machine and learn to be as lazy and self-indulgent as the next citizen. Maybe we all hit a point in our lives where we have to run. We just have to get out there and see what there is then we can worry about sitting at home. Maybe this will be me someday; especially after this race... maybe not. For now, this is my relaxation and what I do for self-indulgent, totally selfish behavior.

As most young men do, I took example from those around me. With so much wanted and desired at that young of an age, it was important for me to be just like them when I grew up. So, I worked a good business, got good people around me, did good things and enjoyed the fruits of my labors. At 27 years of age; I weighed 350 pounds. I also had high blood pressure and high sugar levels. My doctor informed me I was much too young to have these issues and if I did not change my ways, my penis would stop working. He gave me a choice; a list of medicines to pick up from the pharmacy or an appointment 30 days later to check my progress. In 30 day at the appointment, I had lost 20 pounds. I had to just make the effort, I had to drop my weight and live a better lifestyle while consuming less. Less food, less comfort, less of everything was my new life goal. I have come a long way since then at a mere 250 pounds these days and I know I still have a long way to go. My road it seems is never ending but I have been fortunate enough to be blessed with good people who have assisted me in the redirection of my life - my road.

I still smoke too many cigarettes and drink too much coffee and that's just a few of my issues. I have to own all of it. If I let any of my issues own me, it's easy for me to freak out wasting my valuable human time and potential. Owning it; will be the process of my effort in all things around me. Also, I need to own a few other things these days like my relationships with people. If a person lets me down, I need to be okay with letting them out of my life, showing them the door as politely, or maybe a rudely, as possible if the occasion calls for all that. If it turns out that I am alone at the end of the day, I need to be okay with that as well. It's all about time these days for me, not money or things - just time. I want more time to travel, explore, invent, re-engineer, recreate and enjoy the good things in life like the company of my children. The company of good friends or a good woman or even several good women is always nice as well. Work is cool and affords me all I have today but, no man ever died wishing he had worked more in life.

And what about alone? To be alone and without other people I love and know around me has never been my idea of a good time. The main reason I don't mind traveling without stopping might have a lot to do with this social anxiety. To sit in a restaurant by myself and eat is not going to work for me. Starving myself a little on a diet of trail mix, beef jerky and fruit is more my style. Maybe it all equals the ability to do good in this arena but in everyday life it can and will cause problems from time to time. How does one fall apart? How does one begin to put themselves back together? I don't remember or see a moment in time when anything fell apart for me. Some races in this life I have lost and some I have won. Stressing moments, like the birth of my daughter, led to a wonderful human being that taught me so much about happiness. Scary moments, like the birth of my son, have led me to even more absolute happiness; teaching me even more patience with people especially when they are little and just like me. My wife left; but it made her a happier person and easier to be around. My skoot stopped; but I was able to fix it and keep going. It all comes down to management I reckon. Management of finding and discovering what makes me; and the people I chose to be around me, happy. As the mechanic that I am; I have had to get good at all this to make a living. Whether it's planned or on the fly; the universe has never given me anything I can't handle no matter how much I might disagree with that statement at the time. No, for me there is no one moment; it's all a blur of emotions and memories that all put together make me who and what I am today and running down my road.

Turnpike Troubadours "7 and 7" *Diamonds and Gasoline,* Bossier City Records, 2010

In a calm, relaxed and tired state of self, I am finding my Zen here on this road. It's all so bright and brilliant. The wind is hitting my face and eyes, a fresh and new feeling that will wear me out after a few hundred miles - but these few miles at the end here are just fine, and a welcomed change for my face and eyes. The skoot bangs along, thunk, thunk, thunk, while the engine whines and sings. The wind whistles in my right ear with music as my left ear hums at high volume, I won't be hearing anything from that ear for a few days and that is okay with me right about now.

Something catches my eye; I look to my right but see nothing. Wait; there it is again. Something that makes very little sense, but I can see it now plain as day. I shake my head and blink. Still there, running next to me, sleek, lean and mean, Geococcyx Californianus, the Californian Earth Cuckoo. That majestic bird running between my skoot and the blades of grass on the side of the road. This roadrunner is keeping up with me and my skoot, just flying with its feet slapping the pavement so fast my brain cannot begin to process it. Those little legs look like wheels flying under that bird.

Some of my earliest memories consist of this view, as my Pops drove all us kids through the California Desert from Riverside to the Colorado River for those weekends of fun and sun. I look to my left; half expecting to see my Pops driving our old Winnebago sitting next to me. My eyes try to well up with tears at that happy memory; my Pops sipping Shasta cola, that big steering wheel swaying back and forth in his arms, kids bouncing all over that old Winnebago. Always driving the long way through Joshua Tree because the scenery was prettier and the roadrunners - oh those roadrunners - were more visible across the landscapes. Pops always had a good time yelling at me when he saw one. I have always caught glimpses of those roadrunners everywhere I go.

With a known top speed of only 27 mph I don't know how this one is keeping up with me, but there he is, if only for a moment in true roadrunner fashion then swoosh - he is off the road. I look back for him, but he is gone, and the coyote is in his place. In full stride; spitting and snarling to catch him. I have been too relaxed in running this race today, shame on me. Time to run and fly like a roadrunner! Run on this road - your road Bob; away from the coyotes of middle age and growing up. I refuse to let any of that catch me right now. Run Bob, RUN!

On highway 1; now nowhere near the ocean as the number might suggest as this is an actual state highway, a blue highway on old maps. That much closer to the finish line of this race, only 60 or so miles to go. Off the red lines of the maps or interstates and onto a blue line, very exciting but I'm not at the finish line yet. At this point, there is that secure feeling of knowing I am so close I could push my skoot to the finish line if needed. I feel and enjoy the hot humid air on my face cooled by my speed. My senses have been way off. My reality is slipping away from me in all the good ways possible. I sip water, thinking it a good idea to splash equal amounts of water onto the back of my front fender so it cools my engine in this heat.

Simon and Garfunkel, "The Boxer" *Bridge Over Troubled Waters,* Columbia Records, 1970

    Damn this machine and I have come a long way in the last several years. My relationship with it and all that it is, and all that it stands for has proven beneficial beyond my wildest reservations. Sometimes things work out for a man like me, like this machine. It was all a lot of research, trial and error with a splash of good management. I can't be thankful enough to this righteous retired cop skoot. A little luck is always involved when it comes to an undertaking such as this illegal, outlaw road racing business or it's all just part of the plan the universe has for me. This is completely and totally comfortable in my book, this is my comfy leather chair in my living room, my absolute Zen. Infinite amounts of tunability even for a man like me. Through my want and desire to compete and survive, I have tuned my machine, my body and my mind enough for this race. Soon it will all be over, and the realization of all that hits me like all the bugs out here are hitting my face now. How much can I keep going, keep moving forward?

    Passing a lot of little towns; Apex, Sanford, Western Hill, Tramway, Cameron, and so on. Places; places with people all living their lives, sitting on their porches, rubbernecking to see what all the noise is coming down the highway as I wave, and they wave back. I have passed 1,000 towns in the last few days I am sure; amazing me, as it always does, with how much is out here on the road. My theory of the gas stations has proven to be very - incorrect. This is the land of little towns and there are gas stations everywhere. I could of just stopped here, but it doesn't matter if I stopped here or 50 miles ago, at this point in the race it is all the same. Just because it all seemed wrong now, doesn't make it wrong then, hindsight is always 20/20.

When one travels; there is no yesterday just forward. Some travel to get away from something, others travel simply to explore. Unfortunately, most travel for destination, to simply get there. Viewing everything in between as just that; the in between. I have heard a man can go into the desert to lose himself. I live in the desert so maybe I am lost all the time but out here, I can really find myself. I may be racing this skoot, but this is where I reset. All the in between are where all the fun is. Soon I will go back to my old house, my work and my wonderful children. It's all the wonderful life I have made for myself, a better me simply from the act of riding my rigid skoot across country on road. The thing is; I know this is the last scheduled race of this kind. The Stampede has gotten too much bad press and poor claims of it being too dangerous which has led it to be too much trouble. Here in its tenth year, it has been decided that it's time for all of this to end. This finish will be the last finish I get to take on this cross-country chopper race. If the wind was not hitting my eyes so much, I am sure I could feel the tears. I want to cry for this fact. The future is bright, who knows what it holds for cross country chopper racing. Anyone anywhere can throw a toothache like this together but damn; how I have enjoyed chasing the Nomad Charlie across this great country of ours.

This highway is long and straight, just glowing at me as the sun starts its long summer set in these long summer days. Damn I am going to miss this. I am looking for a Best Western Hotel that I think should be up here on the left somewhere if I remember correctly. I have entered the town of Southern Pines,

North Carolina and I know the hotel is somewhere in this little town here on this blue highway. Knowing where I am, here on the other side of the country, is always a weird feeling but I am glad my memory is still working after the last few days. My time has to be pretty good but damn I have been moving slow today as; wait... shit! I hit the brakes without slowing; I hit them harder and the back of the skoot goes into a skid as I try to get into the center turning lane. I separate my tired body from the skoot to push it where it needs to go as the rear end howls and screeches back at me. At this point I can see the road trying to eat me in my side vision, but I keep my head up straight working hard to keep myself upright on my skoot. Damn I am just too damn tired for this right now. Releasing the back brake a little, I stop. There is the hotel, and its driveway, several feet behind me. I make the bitch of a U turn, pulling in and park behind a few competitors skoots that are right in front of the hotel. Hitting the kill switch; the key goes off, the kickstand slams to the pavement as I hurdle off the skoot and through the automatic front doors, straight into a ghost town of a lobby.

 I look around but no one else is here. I stop for a minute, remove my gloves and helmet and start looking for somebody, anybody. I stop to listen but hear nothing, just the hum in my left ear. I have to start to wonder if this is some kind of bad dream. There are no sexy hot threesomes involved so this can't be a dream. This has to be real. I am here, with no one else around.

#24

Passing moments of pure torture, I'm looking around for a piece of paper, I think I have to sign on a piece of paper but damn I can't remember right now. I stink to high hell. I remove my headwrap and slip it into my pocket. Finding a breath mint, I slowly unwrap it, pop it, and start to wonder; I am simply in the wrong place? There are other machines outside, but I did not pay too much attention to them. Maybe they are not other Stampede machines? I put my head down and stare into my helmet; the feeling of defeat is real, but I have come this far, and it seems I may need to go farther to complete this race. Fuck Bob, FUCK!

A voice, I think I hear a voice. I look up to see a young woman making her way out from a door behind the counter. She is talking to someone behind the door and does not see me; slowly starting to move her way. She looks over and sees me; "Well hello there Sir, welcome to the Best Western, what can I do for you?"

"Ahhh," is all I can muster out of my mouth. For several seconds, she stares at me smiling with a look of question. She finally comes around to the counter looking over it at my attire then asks me; "Are you looking for this dear?" As she pulls a slip of paper from her side of the counter. She slaps a map of the

U.S.A. in front of me, the same map I have been following for days and on the other side is the rooster I need to sign.

"Yes!" I expel with a great sigh of relief. I turn it over on the counter and can see the lineup of all who have completed in front of me. I start reaching around my vest, pounding at my pockets.

"Do you have a pen by chance?" I ask her.

"Why yes Sir, uhm, right here."

I sign, next to number 11: Bob Marshall #27 then adding my Flying Marshall Racing Emblem, 8:37 pm 6-16-2015. This takes a ton of effort and concentration as my hands are fighting me. I breathe and do my best to work with them.

As I do this, the familiar voice of my friend and fellow Stampeder Ray comes up behind me, he sets a hand on my back to steady me in my actions of writing. "Bob, how are you doing buddy?" Ray asks.

"Oh, jeez Ray, it's been one hell of a road. I see you came in second place, well done Sir!"

"Well it's good to see you too Bob and you look good. Wow you made good time compared to last time we ran this race. Is everything working okay for you? How do you feel? Do you need anything right now?"

"Thanks Ray but, I was hoping to get in the top 10, but signed number 11. Not bad out of all our competitors but a little behind what I was hoping for, and food please!"

"Bob, there is food everywhere, and read that list again, you will notice everyone signed a line but some finished together; at the same time. Like Pete and Jen, and those corn feed boys from Iowa. Bob, you have finished in 9th place."

"Pete and Jen beat me?" I smile as I say this. Well damn, of course they beat me.

I have to give Ray a lot of credit. As a fellow competitor he knows right now my mind is trying to catch up with my current reality of stopping and finishing this race. My body is sick, and most likely injured but pure adrenaline has been covering it up and now when my mind figures out I am safe and in a declared sanctuary; my body will start to expose all its issues. This will most likely cause me to be sick in one way or another, again.

"Hello Bob." a cool feminine voice states from behind me. "Nice of you to finally join us." Jen and Pete both stroll in the front door as if they were walking on air. Clean and fresh looking but, sunburnt and red as devils with blood shot eyes.

I laugh and smile as they both lose posture. They start explaining how important it was for them to finish in front of me after my comment about beating them. They had finished a few hours earlier, showered, changed clothes and walked to the lobby as they saw me pull up. They have been awake for days and now, can't sleep. I reckon neither can I for that matter.

2 days, 11 hours and 37 minutes, or 59 hours and 37 minutes. is my final time, just under 2 and a half days and just under 3000 miles. 17 hours and 17 minutes behind the first-place finisher Chris Schreiber. Chris is a lean, middle aged hard competitor in this who has finished first before. At a time of 43 hours and 20 minutes. Ray has a few years on all of us in his early 60s but finished a very close second.

The lady behind the counter sets the roster on the counter with a piece of tape to assure my confusion does not happen to the next competitor. I ask her if I can check into the room I had reserved only to be informed that my room is not available. I am a day early for my reservation. I start to pay for another room only to have Ray offer the other bed in his room to me for the night

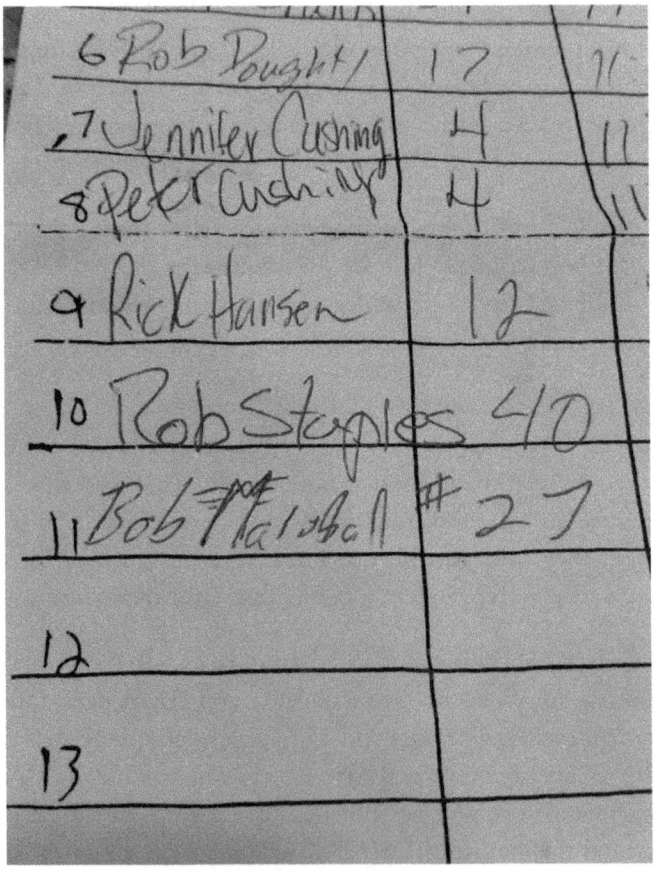

It feels good to be done with this race for now, I ask everyone, "Who's hungry?"

"I'm thirsty."

"Yeah I'm hungry."

"Damn I could eat."

We all march across the street, dodging traffic to one of those wing restaurants. We eat enough to kill a small child while we share stories of the race and compare notes on our road. Also catching up on questions like: where the hell is the Nomad - Charles Davis and why has he not finished the race yet? Why are we all eating and chatting and not sleeping? How did Chris finish just 43 minutes in front of Ray? Is there a larger vessel to carry ranch dressing for dipping our wings? How are Pete and Jen still married after going through the last few days, together? Where are the Miyagi's? How did "Slow Bob" finish before them? Has anyone been to the strip club down the street and do we all want to go there now? Are any of us going to be land sick anytime soon? Lucky for us the establishment had high top tables as most of us stood up, our bums just too sore to sit for a while.

It would turn out Charlie had some electrical issues and while fixing that, broke a bolt on his engine. The Miyagis would finish just under an hour after me, their skoots next to mine as we all made our way across the highway dodging traffic again. The side story to them was they did compete separately until Mr. Miyagi pulled over on a side road to the side road in the middle of nowhere last night for no reason other than to catch a little nap. When he did this; there was his wife, asleep next to her skoot. He simply cuddled up next to her, somehow finding her in the middle of this race, in the middle of this country. They had to finish together at that point.

After gathering my bag and securing my skoot, I sit there for a minute; starring and just totally marveled at all this machine has been through. All it has done for me and all we have done together. "Maybe you deserve a name after all of this my dear friend." Patting the tank, I head to Ray's room and proceed to get the best 10 hours of sleep my body could ever ask for, dirty and all.

#25

I woke up the next day around noon, dazed and sore. I really had to pee; it was time to start moving again. I have not popped any pain pills yet; just gonna let my body ride this one out on its own. I showered, cleared out of Rays room and checked into mine, taking note of all the skoots in the parking lot that had finished including Grandpaw's. I then hit the local Walmart for some new shirts as the ones I brought were a little heavy and long sleeved, perfect for racing cross country, bad for hot humid southern weather. A few undershirts should be fine. I rode down a few blocks only to see Jer, one of the Jack brothers, a fellow competitor.

Jer smelled really bad. He was clean, or looked clean, with his long beard and long hair but his clothing was not. He apologized profusely, not only does he look like a bum but now he smelled like one as well. Apparently, his backpack of clothing flew off his skoot somewhere in the middle, so he had been wearing the same clothing for the entire race. Now as we shuffled down the aisles and he purchased new clothing I kept my distance. Enjoying the reactions of other patrons as he walked by them. Lucky for me Jer is loud and projects when he speaks so I could hear his tales about his road and his complaint on the price of underwear. I remind him he could go without underwear but to each man their own. He bought the undies. He was covered in grease and road dirt as most of us are at the end of this race, he had good reasons and stories of fixing this or that, as he is one hell of a mechanic, and he finished behind me.

Apparently, the sinking feeling he got when he saw on social media that I, "Slow Bob" had finished the race was priceless. He threw up his arms in disgust, pissed off, proclaiming the race was over. Then jumped on his skoot and hauled arse to the finish line. Jer was the one to give me my new nick name as he had passed me several times, a little sore that I had ridden by him early in the race, waving and smiling when he was broken down on the side of the road somewhere in the middle of nowhere. Racing is racing, Jer is a talented man, I knew he would figure it out without me. Slow and steady won the race over Jer on this one. I am glad to know we can all have such psychological effects on each other when we have not slept in a few days, then laugh about it all later.

F Bomb would finish just 25 hours after me, complete in one piece with his little 250 engine still intact, 31st to sign the rooster. I just have to marvel; I mean who the heck pushes an old rebel 250 engine across country; twice? Damn that dude is awesome!

A few hours before he finished, his girlfriend Heather would arrive after a plane ride into Raleigh and meet Ella who also just flew in. While rewiring and mounting some new taillights onto my skoot in the parking lot of the hotel they would pull up and Ella would sneak up behind me, embracing me. What a great compliment to have this woman fly across country to hang out with little ole' me.

Several days of rest, relaxation, eating, and sexual debauchery would follow. A day of chasing around for a new rear tire would lead Ella and me on some wonderful roads, with green everywhere and the wind in our faces. After a few bad leads I would eventually find one at the funniest motorcycle store in some little town where the owner and operator allowed me to assist him in putting on the new rear tire that he sold to me for a pretty penny.

Have you ever tried to handle the most nomadic tribe on the planet? We all would do our best to gather and take a ride that Saturday morning for a photo shot with photographer Michael Lichter. I am sure everyone has seen his work as he has been at this photography thing for a long time and captured some of the great moments of our infamous biker lifestyle. He sat astride the back of a skoot backwards and took pics of us as we rode on past him.

We also had a brief run in with the local law enforcement who pulled us all over after a car had side swiped a fellow competitor, Beardo. His name is Chris, but we call him Beardo, if you ever get the chance to meet him, his dreaded hair and beard speaks for itself. So there we all were, in the empty parking lot of the local insane asylum sitting around waiting for the local Chief of police to figure out that this car had side swiped Beardo and when the driver of the vehicle would not communicate with any of us, we all just left. Beardo had no injuries, just a bent foot peg. The Chief of police made a few phone calls after getting our side of the story, including to her daughter who happened to manage the Best Western, the same lady who I met when finishing the race. She vouched for us that we all may look a little ratty and dirty, but we were all terribly polite and the Chief, 'Mom,' should believe what we say. On that note, the tall bulky man of an officer standing next to me asked if he could take a selfie. After a few good photo moments including the chief pretending she was arresting Beardo on the hood of her cruiser, we were given a police escort to assure no other vehicles would be harming us as we went back to our photo shot on the road. Always a good time with local law enforcement and a Motley Crew of cross-country chopper racers.

One of our fellow competitors Mike Shoup would finish a day behind me after blowing a tire and waiting all night for the Honda dealership to open. He would get an earful from everyone on where his dad was. His dad, Richard, had decided to compete in the race as well and by the 5th day no one had heard from him as he did not own a cell phone. Mike kept reassuring us all he would be fine, and he will be here soon enough. What badassery of an example to us young'uns; I mean even Grandpaw has a flip phone, but to compete in the Stampede without a phone at all? Seems Mike and the rest of us could learn a few things from a man like Richard Shoup.

The Smoke Out chopper show was as cool as it could be for how hot it was that weekend and Saturday night all us Stampeders would get up on the main stage to be rewarded with our patches and our trophy to Chris with Charlie leading the ceremonies as usual. Although the cheers, and wishes of congratulations are always appreciated, people like us who competed in this race do it for other reasons.

To find one's road, one must get out on the road; make a few wrong turns and deal with a few breakdowns. Enjoy all the weather both good or bad, hot or cold, dry or wet. When racing cross country on a motorcycle, it's all road. It will be your best friend or worst enemy, and it's all up to you which one it is. Life is so damn short and for all us racers, finding our own road across this country with our home-built machines is mostly what it's all about. With all the good to come from completing a task such as the Stampede, the universe would remind us all just how short life could be.

One of our last nights there, I stepped out of the hotel room late at night for a smoke after making love to Ella. As I stood there half naked and tired, I heard what I though was a car hitting the curb or something. It sounded terrible but I did not hear too much commotion afterwards and assumed it would all get figured out. Tired and wasted from the day and evening, I crawled back into bed, curled up to Ella and wrapped my tired hands around her large breasts.

The next morning, I got an early call from F Bomb's girlfriend as she explained the situation. The accident I heard last night was our friend Richie Pan and his co-worker Michael Napolitano being stuck by a car as they were crossing the highway. Richie was a tattoo artist and did some pretty righteous work on skoots as well and also a good friend of F Bomb. Everyone was just in shock, losing a friend and fellow rider was a very real reminder on just how short this life really is, for all of us. I personally had just gotten to meet Richie the day before, and damn he rode one hell of a sweet old pan Harley. May you both - Ride in Peace - gentlemen.

My road, running on my road for me is always about - self. It's about unplugging for a moment and doing something so far out of the normal that most people don't even believe me. When they figure out what the race is and that I have competed in it, the realization sometimes is too much for most to handle, and that's okay.

I, Bob Marshall; am a Stampeder. I have purposely rebuilt a perfectly good cop bike into a chopper just to beat the shit out of it, and have it beat the shit out of me, all the way across this country. All illegally, immorally, and against all better judgment.

There are only 150 or so of us Stampeders, all scattered around the world. All from different walks of life with different ideas of cool and reasons why we competed in this race. Some of us are still great friends using any opportunity to ride a thousand miles just to hang out, usually around chopper shows of one kind or another. There is very little I would not do for a fellow Stampeder as I know there is very little they would not do for me.

#26

With so many miles from here to there and so many miles left to bear. To the next petrol station, I roll on, without a normal human care.

-- Bob Marshall

    I have always been able to view my life as a road. Sometimes bumpy, wicked and twisted, slippery when wet, burning when hot. But it is on the road I learn to run and all the freedoms that come with that as well as the consequences for those freedoms. Some people stop on their own road at a certain point for one reason or another. Some pick the easiest and smoothest roads and run only during good weather. Every day we all will have to choose to ride and run on our own road.

Willy Tea Taylor, "Young When I Left Home," *Born and Raised,* independently released 2012

    I am always thankful for all the bumps and sucker punches the road dispatches to me and my aging body. The pain that follows always reminds me that I am alive. The wet, the totally smooth and the weather both good and bad. The curves, the banks and the straights, whatever the road may bring for me it is mine to claim, my road to run, always moving forward. With all the universe has put me through, it has made me the human man I am today. It all forces me, enables me, to learn who I am as a Road Runner. The closer and closer I get to the finish line, the more I want to keep running, learning and growing. We all have a path, a destination; my chosen path will always be as Road Runner.

Several months later my relationship with 'her who shall no longer be named' would come to an abrupt and sudden end. After she moved into my home, we would have a good routine living life and all that domestic partnership has to offer. Enjoying our family time together, children, riding, racing, sexual play and friendships with other women, and above all the joy of each other's company and communication. One day she would tell me in a phone call that she would be home early from work as I was planning to be home early as well. We would say we loved each other as we usually do. I would hang up then never hear from her again.

After several hours of waiting for her, I had to assume she just needed some time away, maybe, I did not know and my mind would wander down dark streets in the middle of a pitch-black autumn night. I had to accept that for some reason she had left and wanted to move on without telling me. She would never tell me; I would never have the human desire for an answer made available. The young woman I fell in love with turned out to be a very little confused girl, a liar, and from what I figured out later; a cheater as well. I would have to do one of the hardest things I have ever done; learn to forgive someone when they never asked for forgiveness. Forgive her for leaving without notice, forgive her for her rudeness in the situation to me and my family. Forgive her for her lying and cheating and above all, forgive myself for allowing anyone to have that much effect on me.

The term I had to learn was called 'ghosting'. It would take me months to learn exactly what this term meant as I never could have imagined the young woman that I loved would simply never communicate with me again and simply, ghost me. Maybe if I was a drunk, or a bum, or physically or verbally abusive all this would make sense. I am none of those things and after hours of talks with my supportive friends and family, I had to learn she was just not brave enough to tell me she wanted to leave our relationship for reasons unknown. Shame on her, the confused irresponsible little girl. The answer to all of it was, my mistress was right.

I would rebuke and ignore the friends and thirds we had had together and learn who I wanted in my life and who I could not live without. Friends would pull close to me reminding me I was good, and life is good. I would try to casually date but with no want or desire for the conflict or drama of all that, it was simply not for me. The great spiritual awakening on who I was would show later on my road, but it would be rough, as rough as rough could be.

I would have to learn to do it my way, I would have to know and accept the universe was, showing me something to better me on my road. My friend Shinya Kimura hangs a big arse tumbleweed in his shop amongst the works of art we call his motorcycles. I learned a lot from him the day I walked into his shop and saw the biggest, greatest, most glorious tumbleweed one could ever imagine, captured from the wind. Admire the little things in life and be thankful for them, appreciate the beauty in everything even, a really big arse tumbleweed. Yes, we are all human, connected by so much I just don't understand or comprehend, but I would have to learn to do it myself, my way, and learn exactly what that meant.

American Road Runner

Many months after she left in the beginning of spring and a forced vacation from any real riding, I would ride my cop chop halfway across country with my friends Twila and her husband Matt. They were so good to me and my family after all they had seen me go though, just true friends. They would invite me, so off we went, like normal riding Americans, spending 3 days riding to a little chopper show in New Braunfels, Texas called 'The Giddy Up'. A very slow, moderate, let's all have a good time along the way, 3 days of riding and camping all the way there, well and a hotel room or 2 of course. I would get to the campsite in New Braunfels a little late in the dark after hanging out with some fellow Stampeders at the local Harley dealership. I would pitch my tent in the dark next to the Guadalupe (pronounced Guadalup) river and fall asleep.

When I awoke early the next morning to the call of nature, I would step out or fall out of my tent, see no one around, walk 5 feet to the riverbank and pee. The water would prove to be very cold and very deep. I would turn around after I finished only to see a woman sitting at a picnic table 10 feet behind me, enjoying her morning coffee, breakfast tacos and, the sight of me peeing in the river. She had to be the most beautiful woman my mind could ever imagine just sitting there; all be it inappropriate for me to think or say it at that time because, she was married. I quickly stumbled over, not offering my hand to shake hers and said, "Good Morning."

"You must be Bob" she would reply, and a wonderful friendship and eventually love affair would ensue in Austin Texas but that as they say; is another story.

Bob Marshall

There are no finish lines, just spaces between the races. My fine ugly mechanical machines will rock me as far as I rebuild them too. With people, all the rules seem to be thrown out the window and the moral and principles of the woman I had been choosing to be involved with could switch, at a moment's notice. I had to learn the hard way that no matter what people tell me, it all can change in a split second, like blowing a tire at 80 miles an hour. As the true mechanic I am in all I do there is usually reason for everything I do and how I do it. This, that I live by and constantly tune inside myself, would prove to be unavailable in that young woman I had chosen to fall in love with. So be it, lessons learned. The bad tire is replaceable, people and the feelings of love and acceptance that others give you; not so much. Communication from other humans has proven to be the most valued and cherished gift I could ever receive as I would learn that receiving it, was rare. I believe all that, led me to where I am today: on MY ROAD, the Road Runner: outsmarting that damn Coyote. Pain dispatched from people is simply just a part of life, and I thank the universe for showing me that. It all reminds me that I am alive, a living breathing member of this human race running on my own roads, constantly tuning myself as one of the many American Road Runners.

#27

"At the end of the highway, there is no place you can go."

--Earl Grant

"The Cop Chop #27"

Sometimes ya just gotta tune yourself enough and do something as crazy as naming a damn machine.

There may not be a place to go at the end of the highway but that is not my destination. My chosen end is out there, somewhere off in the distance sitting on that beautiful horizon and I have a lot of life left in me to catch it.

The End – For Now

The Author

The only way to keep up with Bob Marshall and all the wrenching, racing, re-building and road running he is doing is to check him out on social media. Also find him on The American Road Runner Motorcycle Show podcast and on the website. The Stampede may be over, but the adventures continue. More books and stories from the road to follow soon.

Find this book narrated by the Author on Audible.

Find the American Road Runner Motorcycle Show where ever you get your podcasts or on You Tube.

Go to and follow:

www.AmericanRoadRunnerTheBook.com

On Instagram, Facebook, Goodreads and You Tube:

American Road Runner

We thank you in advance for leaving a rating and review.

Bob Marshall

EMERGENCY ROAD PAPER
COMPLIMENTS OF THE AUTHOR:
BOB MARSHALL

American Road Runner

EMEGENCY ROAD PAPER
COMPLIMENTS OF THE AUTHOR:
BOB MARSHALL

Bob Marshall

EMEGENCY ROAD PAPER
COMPLIMENTS OF THE AUTHOR:
BOB MARSHALL

American Road Runner

EMEGENCY ROAD PAPER
COMPLIMENTS OF THE AUTHOR:
BOB MARSHALL

Bob Marshall

American Road Runner

www.ingramcontent.com/pod-product-compliance
Lightning Source LLC
Chambersburg PA
CBHW071000160426
43193CB00012B/1854